Inventing Greenland

Designing an Arctic Nation

Bert De Jonghe

Contents

Imagining Greenland

Charles Waldheim

Inventing Greenland offers a timely contribution to the growing literature on Arctic studies in design as well as an important chapter in the description of planetary urbanization. De Jonghe's texts, maps, and photographs assemble an intelligent, thick description of a territory that has remained on the periphery of our awareness and understanding. This publication brings into view a fascinating case study of the contested claims, competing agendas, and contrasting futures of the place and its people.

In his 1855 map of "British, Russian & Danish Possessions in North America" (Fig. 1), New York cartographer Joseph Hutchins Colton depicted Greenland as a Danish colony on the extreme northeastern edge of North America. Colton's depiction of contested colonial claims across the northern frontier of the continent reveal a contested Arctic, one in which various European imperial states sought to project their own futures across a vast and extreme landscape. Rather than depicting Greenland as an autonomous island (for some, the world's largest) in the North Atlantic, Colton chose to see Greenland as imbricated in the geographic, political, and cultural conditions of the North American Arctic. Colton reinforced this reading by neglecting to include Greenland in his now canonic "Comparative Sizes of Islands and Lakes" (Fig. 2), published in the same *Colton's Atlas of the World,* which featured the Danish colony as a remote hinterland in the European colonization of the Americas.

Rather than a naturally occurring condition, geography, or geology, Greenland was made up. It was invented, so to speak, by various peoples over various eras, each projecting their own fantastically radical vision of this place and its potentials. Before Greenland could be invented, it first had to be imagined. In this case, the map preceded the territory, just as the name preceded the map. Even the name itself was a lie, or a marketing misdirection at the least, the first fabulation among many over centuries of attempts to imagine Greenland by remote cartographers and colonizers. Of course, the first humans to occupy what we now describe as Greenland had no conception of such an entity. The ancestors of the Inuit populations who now make up most of the island's population settled on the southwestern edge of the great island of ice half a millennium after Norse settlers had done the same. Since that time, the geographic and political entity described under the name Greenland has been subject to various claims from European, North American, and Asian cultures seeking to construct its future in their own image.

No small part of the compelling quality of the story told here has to do with the relative remoteness of the territory as well as the extremity of its conditions for human habitation. Despite its extremity, Greenland has been imagined in very different ways by European, North American, and Asian imaginations. Because of its extremity, Greenland has, to date, persisted in a resilient state of ambivalent resistance to all but the most ambitious and durable of these various interventions. These various contested claims have reimagined Greenland as a site for resource extraction, strategic military advantage, shortened shipping routes, exotic touristic amenities, airport urbanism, and postcolonial self-governance. *Inventing Greenland* reveals these various contested histories and interested futures through a close reading of the infrastructure supporting each of these visions and the forms of urbanization that they portend. In so doing, this publication sheds important light on a territory that has for too long remained on the margins of our maps and in the margins of our imagination.

Charles Waldheim is John E. Irving Professor of Landscape Architecture at the Harvard University Graduate School of Design where he directs the Office for Urbanization.

Fig. 1. J.H. Colton, "British, Russian & Danish Possessions in North America," *Colton's Atlas of the World Illustrating Physical and Political Geography* (New York: J.H. Colton, 1855).

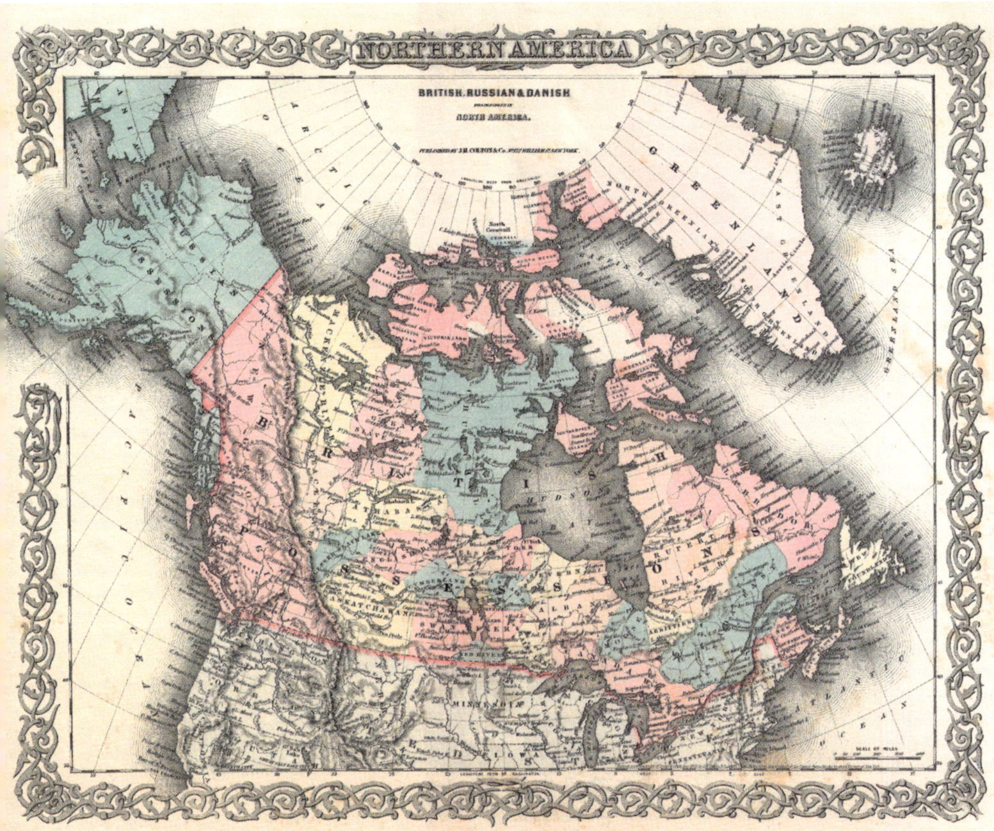
NORTHERN AMERICA
BRITISH, RUSSIAN & DANISH
NORTH AMERICA.
GREENLAND
RUSSIAN POSSESSIONS
BRITISH POSSESSIONS
HUDSON BAY
ARCTIC OCEAN
PACIFIC OCEAN
ATLANTIC OCEAN
MINNESOTA

Fig. 2. J.H. Colton, "Comparative Size of Lakes and Islands," *Colton's Atlas of the World Illustrating Physical and Political Geography* (New York: J.H. Colton, 1855).

COMPARATIVE SIZE OF LAKES & ISLANDS
LAKES IN THE WESTERN HEMISPHERE
LAKES IN THE EASTERN HEMISPHERE
ISLANDS IN THE WESTERN HEMISPHERE
ISLANDS IN THE EASTERN HEMISPHERE
LAKE SUPERIOR
LAKE MICHIGAN
LAKE HURON
LAKE ONTARIO
WINNIPEG
ATHABASCA
GREAT SLAVE LAKE
GREAT BEAR LAKE
BLACK SEA
CASPIAN SEA
SEA OF ARAL
LAKE BAIKAL
LAKE NYASSI
NEW FOUNDLAND
CUBA
JAMAICA
ST. DOMINGO
VANCOUVER I.
ICELAND
BRITISH ISLES
ENGLAND
IRELAND
SICILY
CEYLON
JAVA
VAN DIEMEN LAND
SARDINIA
CORSICA

Introduction

Numbering only 56,400 residents, Greenland's population is dispersed throughout a large number of settlements scattered across a vast area. As an enormous ice sheet covers 80 percent of Greenland's land surface, people live along the rugged shorelines, mostly in the western region—a thin strip of habitable land stretching from Qaanaaq in the north (77°46'N) to Nanortalik in the south (60°14'N). The story of Greenland's settlement and urbanization processes is complex. While Danish colonists instrumentalized urbanization in Greenland as a means of imprinting and managing their culture onto a seemingly unruly society and landscape, today, urbanization offers a means of fostering more bottom-up, inclusive nation-building. Within this larger narrative, other actors such as the US military also play a significant role. Therefore, as an unconventional entry into understanding urbanization processes in Greenland, the reader is first introduced to the topic of American interventions and influences.

The first chapter, "Militarization and Globalization," describes how Greenland's airspace, air routes, and airports—collectively referred to as an "aeroscape"—were constructed to meet the needs of American military colonialism (Heymann et al. 2010) rather than those of Greenlanders. This practice of military colonialism has highly impacted processes of urbanization and nation-building in Greenland. Interventions in Greenland's aeroscape are bracketed into three periods, which reflect contemporaneous processes experienced across the wider Arctic: (1) militarization and the production of Greenland as an airspace; (2) decolonization, the development of Air Greenland, and the production of Greenland as a nation; and (3) self-rule, globalization, and the production of Greenland as a destination for tourists and magnet for foreign investment. This periodization helps explain why contemporary plans to redevelop

Greenland's aeroscape and reorient it within global, rather than domestic, networks threatens to disconnect local settlements whose airports have been targeted for closure in an effort to rationalize the national air transportation system. This chapter therefore calls for more attention to the afterlife of infrastructure and the consequences of excluding communities whose origins lie in previous military and colonial interventions from postcolonial nation-building projects.

Following the interconnected story of airports and settlements in Greenland, the next chapter, "Shared Histories and Collective Memories," goes back in time to provide an additional historic perspective regarding Greenland's urbanization. Drawing on mostly historical and anthropological research by Scandinavian scholars, this chapter covers the rise and fall of the Greenland Vikings, the migration of Inuit hunting tribes from the Arctic shores of North America to northwest Greenland, the ramifications of Danish colonialist policies to "modernize" (or more precisely, further "Westernize") both the country and Inuit society, and finally, the lengthy process of decolonization with the introduction of Home Rule in 1979 and Self Rule in 2009. This policy background is overlaid against an exploration of the intimate matrix of connections between Inuit culture and the local landscape resulting in an architecture and lifestyle adapted to the seasons, the availability of food, and more. Through this analysis, this chapter demonstrates that, to date, urbanization in Greenland has largely been a foreign process difficult to map onto preexisting semi-nomadic and communal ways of living. Incorporated into this argument is a brief description of unique map-making practices and encounters with foreign explorers. While mapmaking served as a product of power and a tool for colonization, with foreigners instrumentalizing Inuit knowledge in order to safely navigate Greenland's extreme landscapes, the practice also fostered collaboration and companionship between foreign explorers and local Inuit.

In the shadow of the many encounters with foreign explorers, whalers, and scientists, Danish colonizers had a more startling impact on traditional Inuit society. These impacts are explored in the third chapter, "Housing and Public Projects," through its discussion of past housing issues produced by Danish policies and European-inspired housing blocks, which are manifested by Block P, an infamous, 200-meter-long, five-story apartment complex in Nuuk, Greenland's capital. Block P exposes Danish urban planners' failure to follow local knowledge and culture, resulting in accommodations poorly suited to the Greenlandic context. Its own shortcomings are representative of other housing and public projects in Greenland. As numerous planning and societal problems persist in Nuuk, this chapter critiques what went wrong with past housing and public projects in order to set the stage for an exploration of contemporary proposals and ideas situated within the surrounding landscape that promisingly emphasize a strong sense of community while empowering local people.

Greenland's housing problems have multiple historical roots stemming from not only the imposition of urban planning schemes from the outside, but also foreign aesthetics and categorization schemes, too. In the 1950s and '60s, the work of Danish architects contributed heavily to a "chromatic geography" (Doherty 2010) of colorful prefab housing typologies in Greenland. Typically, the color schemes of Greenland's built environment have embodied a Danish colonial approach, codifying and controlling the country's resources and urban landscapes. Besides color, the scarcity of wood as a building material also influenced Greenlandic architecture during Danish colonialism. Timber, among other construction materials, had to be shipped to Greenland from Scandinavia. Today, Greenland still relies to a great extent on the outside world for building materials. To consider possibilities for breaking from this foreign color coding and the dependence on the outside world for urban construction, the fourth chapter, "Chromatic Geographies and Material Economies," reflects upon the history and meaning of such practices and the potential for them to be transformed.

The final chapter, "Arctic Tourism and Urban Growth," explores the town of Ilulissat, one of the main actors in the ongoing reorganization of Greenland's aeroscape. Ilulissat's airport expansion offers a useful case study for examining the town's historic and potential future growth resulting from the new airport and the town's increasing numbers of tourists. This process is also highly intertwined with Ilulissat's neighboring ice fjord and glacier, which propel the tourism industry in the city and in the broader region. The near-continuous calving of the glacier front undergirds the town's unique relationship to dynamic ice in an urban setting. The large icebergs, however, have long been seen as so sublime that their aesthetic value has been privileged over Ilulissat's urban landscape and local culture, leading tourists to expect an "untouched and human-free landscape" (Smed 2017). This chapter argues that designers can play an important role in translating Ilulissat's complexity—including a continued and careful consideration of the nature/culture relationship, embracing Ilulissat's urban connection with the ice and navigating sustainable growth of Ilulissat's built environment.

The book's conclusion synthesizes and connects the arguments presented in the previous five chapters. By underscoring that the idea of Greenland comprises a wide range of perspectives, histories, and forces, including a long history of inhabitation spanning across many centuries, cultures, and rapidly changing climates, it acknowledges the historic impacts and future potential of the book's main focus: urbanization.

Acknowledgments

I am neither from Greenland nor Denmark, but Belgium. My first research trip to Greenland (Kangerlussuaq, Nuuk, Kulusuk, and Tasiilaq) was in 2017, followed by extensive research, including archival research, publications, conference presentations, multiple interviews with both Greenlandic and Danish people, and many discussions with academics and mentors. Generous support from the Penny White Project Fund (Harvard University, 2020) allowed me to conduct additional on-site research in Narsarsuaq, Nanortalik, and Qaqortoq. This trip, however, was postponed due to the COVID-19 pandemic. In the summer of 2021, one final visit was conducted to Kangerlussuaq, Nuuk, Oqaatsut, and Ilulissat. This book project was also fortunate to be intellectually supported by copyeditor Mia Bennett's two field visits to Greenland in 2014 and 2017. The combination of field visits, extensive research, and persistence resulted in two master theses—at the Oslo School of Architecture and Design (AHO) in 2018 and the Harvard University Graduate School of Design in 2021—and finally this book project.

Many of the early investigations were carried out to observe, understand, and ask questions, rather than reinforce preexisting beliefs or preconceptions. A fixed or predetermined point of view would only lead to a singular history/future, instead of unraveling multiple and nonexclusive histories/futures (Eigen 2020). In other words, I have approached every visit, conversation, situation, and story with an open mind, allowing myself to unlearn and learn. As a result of this approach—and differing from dominant narratives and histories in Western scholarship—this book aims to push back against situating Greenland on the frontlines of climate change and between great power politics with little attention to its internal dynamics. Such representations also make the mistake of reducing "the place of Greenland to just one component of an abstract cryosphere" (Billingsley 2020). Although the book's approach is multifaceted, it does not pretend to include everything.

During the research and writing process, I was privileged to gather many rich insights from both Greenlandic and Danish people, who helped shape my understanding of Greenland as a complex cultural, interconnected, and geographical space. One of my underlying hopes is to share this perspective and eventually contribute to the reframing of existing narratives. Therefore, it is essential to know what those narratives are, to position them in time, and to explore ways to collectively move forward. Taken as a whole, this book can be understood as an invitation to continue fostering a constructive conversation about Greenland's built environment.

I am grateful to the many people who have contributed to the process of realizing this book. Special thanks to Charles Waldheim for his guidance, mentorship, and support from start to finish. Many thanks to Mia Bennett for the co-authorship of this book's chapter "Militarization and Globalization," as well as for her editorial advice, copyediting, and intellectual stimulation overall. Thanks to the American Association of Geographers (AAG) for giving me the opportunity to present this book's "Chromatic Geographies and Material Economies" at its annual meeting on April 9, 2021. Thank you to the International Congress of Arctic Social Sciences (ICASS X) for providing a platform to share and discuss this book's first chapter—then referred to as "Geopolitics at the Gates: The Militarization, Decolonization, and Globalization of Greenland's Aeroscape"—on June 20, 2021. Thanks to Mason White (Lateral Office), Leena Cho (Arctic Design Group), Peter Hemmersam (AHO), Igor Marjanovic, and Alex Wall for their insightful comments during my Harvard GSD Thesis review in May 2021. Thanks to Danielle Choi, Kira Bre Clingen, and Adriana Pablos Llona for their helpful comments and support during monthly MDes thesis working sessions. Thank you to the people I have met on my travels to Greenland, both in-person and virtually, including Aganni Peter Mathiassen, Maja, Jan, Søren, Dennis, Fredrik Wille, Justine Wille, Anders Østergaard, Jesper Postas Krogh, Morten Mikkelsen, Matt Spenceley, Klaus Georg Hansen, Qivioq Nivi Løvstrøm, Nive

Nielsen, Inuuteq Holm Olsen, Runa Sværd, and many more. Thank you to the people whom I met at Harvard University and who have supported directly or indirectly early versions and parts of this project, among others: Alex Wall, Antoine Picon, Jesse M. Keenan, Jeffrey S. Nesbit, Halla Hrund Logadóttir, Blake Mitchell, Yvonne Fang, Susan S. Fainstein, Robert Gerard Pietrusko, Greg Poelzer, and Joel Clement. Thank you to the people at the Oslo School of Architecture and Design: Thomas Juel Clemmensen, Annie Breton, Eimear Tynan, Marianne Lucie Skuncke, Mari Bergset, Luis Callejas, Janike Kampevold Larsen, Kjerstin Uhre, Knut Eirik Dahl, Brona Keenan, Nick Gulick, Marta Kováčová, Élisabeth Baril, Victoria Cobeña Serrano, Kathrine Omnia Strøm, Björn Ekelund, and many others. Thank you to Elizabeth Kugler, Stig Søndergaard Rasmussen, Visda, and Sabam for their administrative support. Thank you to the Danish Arktisk Institut and the contributing photographers (Bent Helmudt, Finn Samson, Jette Bang, Svend Lauge Koch, Therkel Mathiassen, David Trood, Aningaaq Rosing Carlsen, Inger Oxholm Campsie, Filip Gielda, Annie Pratt, Adam Mork, Jon Arnold, and Dirk De Jonghe) for their inspiring visual input. Thank you to Ricardo Devesa and his team at Actar Publishers and urban-Next for distributing this work to a broader audience. Thank you to my parents, family, and friends.

Greenland's towns and settlements are in direct relation to the ice flow of the Greelandic Ice Sheet.

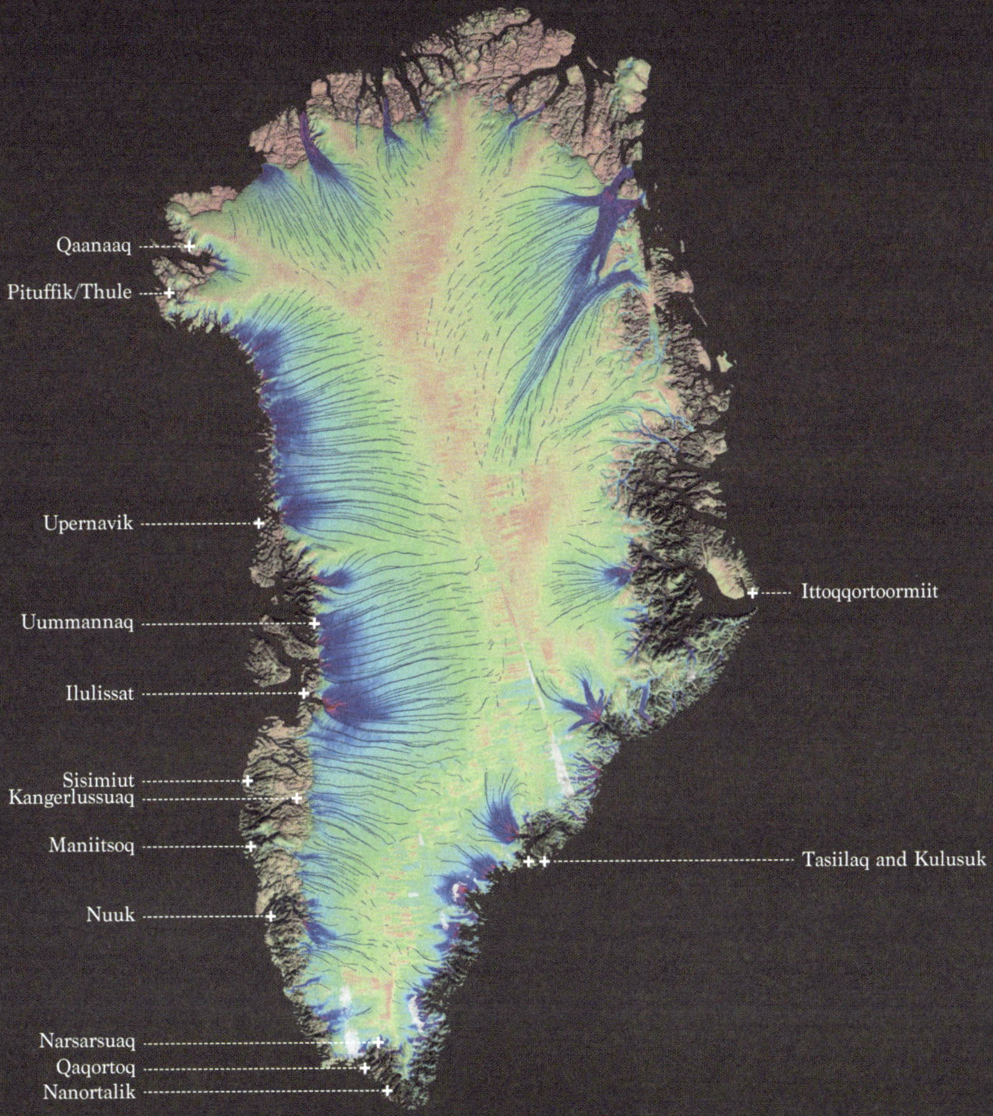
Qaanaaq
Pituffik/Thule
Upernavik
Uummannaq
Ilulissat
Sisimiut
Kangerlussuaq
Maniitsoq
Nuuk
Narsarsuaq
Qaqortoq
Nanortalik
Ittoqqortoormiit
Tasiilaq and Kulusuk

Militarization and Globalization

Mia Bennett and Bert De Jonghe

Much has been published about *the* history of Greenland—or Kalaallit Nunaat, meaning Land of Greenlanders or Land of the People in Greenlandic (Kaae 2006). However, it is the authors' intention to weave together a more diverse array of studies and stories in order to drift through *a* history of Greenland or, more ambitiously, several *histories* (Eigen 2020). Such an approach helps reveal Greenland as a palimpsest and encourages the reader to perceive Greenland as a complex and interconnected cultural and geographical space rather than as a remote, barren, and sparsely populated periphery. One point of entry to Greenlandic histories is the topic of Greenland's airspace, air routes, and airports—collectively referred to as "aeroscape"—in relation to local communities, urbanization, and nation-building. While modern airports anticipate "the city of the future," according to Dutch architect Constant Nieuwenhuys (Dümpelmann and Waldheim 2016, 16), in Greenland, they may anticipate an independent nation.

Greenland's aviation infrastructure

In less than half a century, transportation in Greenland has shifted from boats and dog teams to a heavy dependence on airplanes and helicopters. In 2019, flag carrier Air Greenland carried 438,000 passengers (Air Greenland 2020), nearly eight times the country's population of 56,400. For comparison, in the US in 2019, all airlines carried 926 million passengers, less than three times the population (Bureau of Transportation Statistics 2020). With 80 percent of Greenland's landmass covered by ice, most of the population lives in settlements concentrated on the thin margin of the west coast, with a handful on the more inaccessible

The US Air Force providing fuel for Kangerlussuaq Airport, 1951.

east coast, too. Waters are mainly navigable from late summer through early fall, while the eastern villages have extremely limited ground access. Compounded by the fact that no two of its eighteen towns or sixty settlements are connected by road, air traffic has become "the sole year-round lifeline for commercial transport and inner-community passenger travel" (Sheppard and White 2017, 280).

Inseparable from Greenlandic airports' logistical role is their social one. The country's fourteen airports serve as places for locals to gather for a hot meal or meet friends and relatives in transit. Despite 9/11 transforming many airports around the world into sterile sites of security theater (Hall 2015), Greenland's airports have managed to maintain their social functions. The buzzy ambience of Greenland's airports is common across the remote Arctic where, in place of roads and highways, airports serve as friendly gathering spots bearing little resemblance to the soulless terminals in cities to the south that speed passengers through to their destinations (Schaberg 2011). Airports are particularly relevant to Greenland's socioeconomic fabric in the locations where they were built by the US during World War II. While these sites were suitable for long-range jets, they initially bore little relevance for Greenlanders. New towns sprang up to support American defense operations in Kangerlussuaq, Narsarsuaq, and Kulusuk. These towns—each of which has no more than a few hundred residents—now depend on airports not only as lifelines to the outside world, but for their own internal social and economic functioning, too.

Greenland's aviation infrastructure is poised to change dramatically in the coming years. In the 2013 film *The Secret Life of Walter Mitty*, the protagonist boards an Airbus A330 direct from New York to the capital of Nuuk. Such a scene is currently confined to the realm of fiction, for Nuuk's short runway can handle only Dash 8 prop planes. Yet this cinematic fantasy may become reality as early as 2023 if the government's plan to move the country's main airport hub from Kangerlussuaq to the capital is realized on time. As part of its pursuit to achieve independence from Denmark and to decrease reliance on the annual block grant it provides, which equals DKK 3.6 billion (US$546 million, equal to 55 percent of government revenue and 20 percent of GDP), the government of Greenland is seeking to attract international flows of capital and people. Airports, with their potential to attract investment and tourists and symbolize the arrival of a "modern" nation, form key sites for realizing a vision of a more independent and globally integrated Greenland. In 2016, Greenland's former prime minister Kim Kielsen remarked that airport expansion "will lead to better and less expensive transport opportunities for our people, while also improving conditions for the development of tourism, commerce, and industry in general" (Naalakkersuisut 2016). Two years later, Greenland's parliament, Inatsisartut, voted (18-9, with two abstentions) to spend DKK 2.1 billion (US$277 million) to renovate existing airports in Nuuk (pop. 17,635) and the UNESCO World Heritage destination of Ilulissat (pop. 4,670) and build a new one in Qaqortoq, the most populated town in southern Greenland (pop. 3,050). While airport renovations may seem a banal issue in many other countries, they are politically freighted in Greenland. The government's ruling coalition collapsed over the vote, as pro-independence party Naleraq quit in opposition to the offer from Copenhagen (with the tacit backing of Washington, DC) to finance the renovations, which it offered allegedly in order to block a bid by a state-owned Chinese enterprise.

Yet behind this geopolitical power-brokering lie more local political consequences, too. As Greenland expands airports in the locations with the greatest potential to attract investment (even if the initial financing still comes from Denmark), this reconfiguration may undermine the settlements that sprang up to support the operations of the country's airports built by the US during and after World War II. Existing hubs like Kulusuk (pop. 241), a former Distant Early Warning Line station that is now the country's eastern air hub; Narsarsuaq (pop. 123), the country's southern hub whose airport will likely be relocated to the larger nearby town of Qaqortoq (pop. 3050); and even Kangerlussuaq (pop. 508), home to Greenland's primary international airport, may be undermined. In situations where towns arose to serve airports rather than the other way around, when an airport is relocated, such alterations to "systems of connection" can threaten not only critical infrastructure but social lifelines altogether (Carruth 2018; Williams 1993). The reorganization of Greenland's aviation infrastructure to support international flows of passengers and capital may come at the cost of the sense of place and purpose in settlements left out of the new nation-building project. It may appear that "the boundaries that fragment terrestrial space disappear in flight, so that space is reduced to a network of points, intersecting lines and altitudinal planes" (Cosgrove 2008, 87). But the making and remaking of airspace, air routes, and airports—"aeroscapes"—in fact constitute a project of territorialization that involves drawing new boundaries both on land and in the air and forming new connections and disconnections between the points holding up the skies.

Radar system at Thule Air Base, 1965.

Militarization and decolonization

Across the Arctic, a great deal of commercial aviation infrastructure has its roots in World War II military operations and their protraction during the Cold War (Farish and Lackenbauer 2009). Although many of these military imperatives have weakened, the path dependency of air transportation networks, which require enormous amounts of fixed capital, makes them difficult to alter. As air power became the key to global military might in the twentieth century, the US started building airstrips and missile defense sites in Greenland in order to safeguard its own national security. American interest heightened following the Nazi invasion of Denmark on April 9, 1940: With Denmark unable to send supplies to Greenland, let alone exercise sovereignty over it, as it had done since the early eighteenth century, the Danish ambassador to the United States, Henrik Kauffmann, disobeyed the Danish government and signed an agreement granting America access to the world's largest island (Rahbek-Clemmensen and Nielsen 2020). In

Air Greenland, Kangerlussuaq Airport, 2021.

addition to civilian resupply and the construction of facilities such as weather stations, ports, depots, search-and-rescue stations, and more, this agreement made it possible for the US to establish military airbases on Greenlandic soil. Greenland's aeroscape was constructed to the needs of American military colonialism (Heymann et al. 2010), rather than those of Greenlanders.

In 1942, the first American airport in Greenland was established at the mouth of Greenland's longest fjord at Kangerlussuaq, which was suitable for a long runway and benefited from fog-free weather. Aside from an intermittent caribou camp little used in the twentieth century, the site appeared to have little local relevance at the time (Grønnow 1986). The closest town, Sisimiut, lies 130 kilometers to the west. With a 1,700-meter-long asphalt runway that was later extended to 3,000 meters, Kangerlussuaq is Greenland's hub for international air traffic and jumbo jets. Economic activity in the settlement of 508 people relies heavily on the airport and the industries that have sprung up around it, involving science, logistics, and tourism.

Later in 1942, another airport was built in Narsarsuaq, located in the relatively fog-free Tunulliarfik Fjord in southern Greenland. Among the locations of the seventeen defense installations built before the war's end (Petersen 2011), Narsarsuaq was unusual in that several settlements were already nearby (the area has a history of habitation that can be traced back to Norse explorer Erik the Red's eastern Viking colony). After the war, in 1956, the American military built a third full-fledged airport on the small, discontinuously inhabited island of Kulusuk to support construction of a radar station (DYE-4) that formed part of the Distant Early Warning Line built from Alaska across Canada to Greenland to warn against Soviet missiles (Elixhauser 2019). Kulusuk followed the typical pattern of constructing an airport in a location far from existing settlements: while a Danish missionary had been established on the island in 1909, other nearby areas offered better hunting grounds, and most of the region's population was based in the town of Tasiilaq twenty kilometers away, on another island (Dzik 2015). Yet as in Kangerlussuaq and Narsarsuaq, in Kulusuk, a settlement directly adjacent to the airport with a couple of hundred people soon grew to support its operations.

While Greenland was returned to Denmark at the war's end, dominating Greenlandic airspace did not suffice for a US government increasingly concerned about the Soviet threat. In 1946, Washington, DC, offered to purchase the island, referred to by the Pentagon as "the world's largest stationary aircraft carrier" (Doel 2016, 29), from Copenhagen for $100 million. While Denmark rejected the proposal, the signing of a bilateral defense agreement in 1951 allowed the US to build a major air base (i.e., Thule Air Base) in northwestern Greenland, where the glacial outwash plain offered a suitable site, along with access to the sea that could enable ships to bring in construction materials and cargo. Construction of Thule Air Base began in 1951 on the outskirts of the Greenlandic village of Pituffik. A lavishly illustrated story in *Life Magazine* in September 1952 introduced American readers to the triumphal story of Thule Air Base's construction, which was

Royal Danish Air Force, Kangerlussuaq Airport, 2021.

considered a technological marvel (Brinkley 1952). *Life* and other media outlets portrayed Greenland as a cultural void and empty land. The US perceived Greenland as a place devoid of culture, where everything had to be imported, modular, and prefabricated (Hemmersam 2016, 416)—a perspective that allowed the military to brazenly relocate entire villages.

As the base expanded to become the second-largest within the US Air Force (Martin-Nielsen 2012), the Danish government forced village residents to relocate 130 kilometers north to a new town called Qaanaaq (Takahashi 2019). They had to move by dog-sled, as the new settlement lacked an airstrip. Dozens of Inughuit (Inuit) households lost their homes. Among them were "veterans from the great expeditions" such as a sixty-four-year-old elder named Odak, who assisted American explorer Robert Peary on his expedition to the North Pole in 1909. But by 1953 the settlements "lay abandoned, and the whole surface of the peninsula [named *Uummannaq*] was scraped and ploughed by bulldozers, so nothing of the original structure remained" (Sørensen 2010, 42). In addition to relocation, in 1968 native Inuit were asked to assist in the cleanup of a crashed nuclear bomber (B-52) in the nearby Wolstenholme Fjord, which included radioactive contamination (Doel 2016, 12). The forced relocation and cleanup highlight the complicated history of Thule Air Base and American influence in Greenland in general. Today, due to the forced relocation, loss of hunting grounds, and more, many Greenlanders and Indigenous and environmental activists dispute the continued prominence of the site and its disruptive historical legacy.

In the 1950s, as American and NATO forces expanded their operations on the world's largest island, transportation demands increased. The development of commercial air routes between North America and Europe via Greenland, Iceland, and northern Canada also opened new opportunities for airport development. In 1953, the change in Greenland's status from a Danish colony to county led authorities to begin developing tourism using two airports constructed by the US military as hubs. In 1958, charter flights began carrying tourists from Iceland to Narsarsuaq, where they stayed in the decommissioned US army barracks. Runways initially developed to support foreign military jets began instead supporting aircraft filled with foreign tourists. The following year, charter flights began carrying tourists from Iceland to nearby Kulusuk, a journey still popular today as a day trip. In the 1960s, SAS (Scandinavian Airlines) began more regularly flying Danish tourists to Narsarsuaq (Tommasini 2014), exemplifying how infrastructure, although contributing to the local economy, still remained oriented to external demands.

Early air routes flown by Air Greenland, a flag carrier established in 1960 (initially as Grønlandsfly), met external, rather than internal, demands. The airline's two initial investors were Scandinavian Airlines (the flag carrier of Denmark, Norway, and Sweden) and Danish mining company Kryolitselskabet Øresund, which after the war took over from the US the strategic cryolite mine outside Ivigtut, in southern Greenland. Although the governments of Greenland and Denmark became shareholders in Air Greenland in 1962, through the 1970s, Air Greenland's routes mainly served military and mining activities scattered around the country, using helicopters and helipads. One destination was the cryolite mine, pejoratively described by a local saying: "Ivigtut is not Greenland." Foreigners traveling by air had easier access to Ivigtut than Native Greenlanders on land, who were allowed to enter the mine site only once weekly to buy imported goods (Berry 2012, 224). Following the establishment of Home Rule in 1979, Greenland's aeroscape was gradually designed to meet the needs of a nascent Greenlandic nation. The transformation of Greenland from a Danish province into an autonomous constituent country of Denmark led the new Home Rule government to invest in building helipads in villages inaccessible by boat in winter and subsidizing air routes to them, improving the supply of food and services (Larsen 1992). In the 1980s, direct flights were established to Iqaluit (the capital of Nunavut, Canada) and Iceland.

The former route was usually empty and was ultimately discontinued due to low demand. So, too, was a direct route between Kangerlussuaq and Baltimore that Air Greenland briefly operated in 2007. Rather than intercontinental commercial air traffic supporting the development of Greenland, as imagined during the early postwar period and as is now once again fantasized, the expansion of the aeroscape to connect Greenland's scattered settlements helped consolidate the country as a functioning logistical space and nation.

Alongside their dramatic impacts to Greenland's social landscape, such as the forced relocations of Inuit settlements, American projects dating back to World War II and the Cold War have also generated major environmental consequences. American photographer Ken Bower documented those environmental atrocities at the former American air base Bluie East Two, a place the local Inuit call "American Flowers." Located in eastern Greenland between the villages of Kuummiut and Sermiligaaq, alongside the Ikateq Fjord, the site consists of 200,000 rusted and leaking oil barrels and old vehicles and structures (Kromann 2019). It operated from 1942 to 1947 and served as a minor US Army airfield to refuel airplanes during an Atlantic crossing. The leaking oil has found its way to the land and water, resulting in a heavily damaged ecosystem and an "unfertile" landscape deprived of hunting and fishing grounds (Elixhauser 2018, 119). In 2018, Greenland's former prime minister Kim Kielsen and the Danish minister of trade and industry Esben Lunde Larsen came to an agreement to clean up the disused military installations and waste at Ikateq (Kromann 2019). The cleanup is expected to take several years. While the Inuit may have had little means to prevent the militarization, which has had drastic and long-term impacts on their lands, with the current Greenlandic and democratic governance system, such practices can now be addressed locally, and the Greenlandic people can prevent or support future interventions through their local representatives.

Housing in Kangerlussuaq, 2021.

Ilulissat Airport and its ongoing runway expansion, 2021.

Ilulissat Airport, 2021.

Self-Rule and Greenland as a destination

In 2008, 75 percent of voters elected to expand Home Rule in Greenland. With increased autonomy and confidence, the government of Greenland is transforming Greenland from a Danish periphery into its own political center (Grydehøj 2014). This transition has engendered the concentration of state resources and infrastructural networks in Nuuk and the development of a global outlook transcending Denmark. Even the country's nation-branding effort, which gained steam following the establishment of self-rule, involves the promotion of tourism, using the slogan "Pioneering Nation" (Thisted 2015). As the government centralizes power and logistics within the country, this new stage in the decolonization process reflects a supplanting of the "geopolitical social" with the "geoeconomic social" (Cowen and Smith 2009). Centers of capital and people within Greenland and even those outside the country's territory will become more closely connected, while small Greenlandic settlements whose aerial infrastructure is deemed irrelevant and unproductive will be disconnected from this new, rationalized aeroscape.

In 2009, the Greenland Self Government appointed a transport commission to recommend changes to the national transportation network. One of their recommendations, which can "prioritize projects according to their economic profitability," is the relocation of Kulusuk's airport to the population center of Tasiilaq, which can currently be reached only by helicopter. This shift, the report states, will save money by lowering the need for helicopter transport and generate "significant benefits for tourists in the area" (Bendsen et al. 2011, 7). There is no mention of the consequences for the settlement of Kulusuk, whose identity in both local and national imaginings is inextricably tied to the airport. When given a piece of paper and pencil, a child in Kulusuk will likely draw "a shieldshaped mountain, then a helicopter and a sun" (Sveinbjörnsdóttir 2015, 35). Greenland's "Pioneering Nation" campaign features a photograph depicting a Kulusuk air traffic controller named Ujarneq Sørensen driving a vehicle at the airport with the tower behind him (Andersen 2016).

The Cold War–era construction of Kulusuk Airport gave rise to a town that existentially depends on it. In an interview, the manager of Kulusuk's sole hotel described the facility as "only here because of the airport." He also described a shift in people's habits away from subsistence activities and toward the market economy:

> **To keep the people in Kulusuk there has to be more job opportunities. People are slowly moving away from hunting and fishing; they need something else.**
> —hotel manager, Kulusuk, 2017

In another interview, a teacher at the local school described Kulusuk's reliance on the airport in more fatalistic terms. When asked about the impacts of the airport's potential closure, she affirmed:

> **Very short answer: if they close the airport—Kulusuk is finished. Kulusuk is dependent on the airport. If they close the airport, it would be very, very bad for the village.**
> —schoolteacher, Kulusuk, 2017

She estimated that if the airport were closed, only 40 to 50 people of the 230 current residents would stay, with the rest moving to Tasiilaq or beyond. A senior airport employee echoed her sentiment. He believes that rather than expand the airport to increase economic stability and the number of jobs, the local Sermersooq Municipality (which was born out of the 2009 reorganization of the country's eighteen municipalities into four and which includes Nuuk all the way on the west coast) wanted people to "move to Tasiilaq or, even better, further west." Reflecting over a hundred years of strained ties between Kulusuk (and east Greenland more generally) and the Greenlandic state, whether based in Copenhagen or Nuuk (Dzik 2015), the airport employee elaborated:

> **I don't think the village is going to grow—West Greenland doesn't want or like East Greenland. That's the problem. Every time if there is something wrong with an aircraft (or something else) they prioritize West Greenland—always. They come with a lot of excuses, sometimes it's the weather, a technical problem, etc. But Air Iceland Connect is always able to land here! It's hard to make something happen in Kulusuk, which is stupid because we have a lot of tourists coming in.**
>
> —senior airport employee, Kulusuk, 2017

In his view, it is the outside—tourists traveling from Iceland, who often come just for one day despite traveling from as far away as Asia (Sveinbjörnsdóttir 2015)—which provides economic stability to this settlement, nicknamed the "Gateway to East Greenland." He also criticized the government's myopic focus on building three airports in west Greenland, especially in foggy Nuuk, which lacks Kangerlussuaq's "perfect flying conditions." He continued:

> **The government of Greenland will never understand. Maybe Kulusuk Airport should become a private airport. Every airport in Greenland is not up-to-date, they don't have the money, we are in a bad cycle. It's also important to give the possibility to the Danish Military to land somewhere—now they can only land in Kangerlussuaq and someplace south. To grow, we need to extend the airstrip and don't use gravel but tar or concrete.**
>
> —senior airport employee, Kulusuk, 2017

His statement points to the paradox of Kulusuk: given the state's supposed desire to close the airport and remove sources of inef-

Kulusuk Airport, 2017.

Tasiilaq Heliport, 2017.

ficiency within Greenland's aeroscape, the only way for the settlement's economy to grow is to deepen military and commercial ties with the outside and perhaps rely more on private, rather than state, investment. Even the airport's material expansion is imagined as necessitating the import of foreign materials like tar and concrete rather than locally sourced gravel.

Kulusuk is a microcosm of Greenland's position in global geopolitics and geoeconomics. As the settlement—and the country—gain independence, they may become more dependent on other countries (Grydehøj 2020) rather than on traditional centers of power, whether Nuuk or Copenhagen. Greenland's aviation development strategy in the 1980s concerned connecting far-flung villages, but now the aim is to simultaneously extend internationally while consolidating domestically. While it has been suggested that Kulusuk be shut down, the runways will be extended in Nuuk and Ilulissat (see chapter 5); at the same time, a new airport will be built in Qaqortoq, and the World War II–era airport in Narsarsuaq will close (Christensen et al. 2020). Greenlandic government documents refer to Nuuk and Ilulissat as "international airports," while Qaqortoq and Tasiilaq are described as "North Atlantic" or "Atlantic" airports, indicating their regional, rather than domestic, orientation. Greenland's national tourist board's tourism plan confirms, "Greenland has, with the decision to build three new airports, chosen to focus wholeheartedly on more tourism" (Visit Greenland 2020, 6).

The Greenland Ministry of Finance's 2020 Political and Economic Report explains that reducing reliance on the Danish block grant necessitates diversifying the economy by "finalising the modernisation of the transport infrastructure serving both passengers and freight with easy and efficient domestic and international mobility" and "improv[ing] Greenland's competitiveness, which can make it more attractive for domestic and foreign businesses to invest" (Ministry of Finance 2020, 6). Seen in this light, the process of seeking greater independence from Denmark may not just necessitate increased dependence on foreign capital: it also may cause the exclusion of small settlements from reconfigured infrastructural networks. What this means for their role within the wider project of Greenlandic nation-building is unclear.

Ironically, the airport expansion in Nuuk and Ilulissat is partly being financed by Copenhagen due to its quest, ostensibly under pressure from the US, to prevent the state-owned China Communications Construction Company, which had bid on the airport expansion contract, from building critical infrastructure in Greenland (Bislev et al. 2018). In light of former US president Donald Trump's professed interest in buying Greenland in 2019 and the US Department of State's announcement in 2020 of a $12.1 million aid package to Greenland and the opening of a new consulate in Nuuk, any investment in and reconfiguration of Greenland's aeroscape must also be considered with respect to the current geopolitical order. The US may no longer be seeking to contain German or Russian expansionism in Greenland but, rather, an ascendant China, which has strengthened its polar capabilities and Arctic activities in recent years. The government of Greenland, too, may seek to capitalize on its renewed geopolitical importance in a warming Arctic by triangulating between powers. In late 2020, negotiations between Greenland, the US, and Denmark regarding a new agreement for Thule Air Base resulted in a new bilateral plan for cooperation between Greenland and the US that may lead to greater trade, investment, and development assistance (Denmark 2020). Regardless of who is financing infrastructure development, given the priorities of the government of Greenland, its immediate consequences may not be new mobilities in unlikely places, but rather the curtailing of mobilities and livelihoods in settlements that have now existed for over half a century.

Narsarsuaq Airport, 2022.

On Kulusuk island, Kulusuk Airport's gravel runway is the only visible infrastructure as seen from outer space.

Shared Histories and Collective Memories

In addition to American interventions impacting Greenlandic settlement localities and futures, urbanization in Greenland is a deeply layered and historically complex construct touching upon many different people and cultures—the Greenland Vikings, Danish colonizers, and the present-day Inuit, among others. They are evidence of the numerous ways of seeing, inhabiting, and navigating the Greenlandic landscape. These notions, however, are influenced by the ability or inability to foster a close relation with, understanding of, and adaptation to Greenland's extreme landscape as well as the attitude to learn from others and share skill sets and stories with the collective.

The Greenland Vikings

The ancestors of the present-day Inuit in Greenland, who make up 89 percent of the country's population, are the Thule Inuit (Lynnerup 2015). Prior to that, archeological findings show evidence of the Saqqaq culture (2500–800 BC), Independence I culture (2400–1000 BC), Independence II culture (700–80 BC), the Dorset culture (500 BC–AD 1500), as well as Norsemen from Iceland, who explored the southwest of Greenland. In 982, approximately three hundred years prior to the Thule Inuit's settlement in Greenland, Eric Thorvaldsson (better known as Eric the Red) was banished from Iceland and led many other disgruntled Vikings to southern Greenland (Doel 2016, 4). According to the Icelandic saga of Eric the Red, Eric is the person who coined the name "Greenland," a moniker promising "verdant pastures and boundless opportunities in a new world" chosen to attract more Norsemen to settle (Nuttall 2017, 27). Residing in two colo-

One of the best-preserved Norse ruins in Greenland is Hvalsey Church, located close to the modern-day settlement of Qaqortoq.

nies called the Eastern and Western Settlements, the Greenland Vikings peaked with around six thousand people and three hundred farms (Doel 2016, 4). They "built manor houses . . . ; they imported stained glass; they raised sheep, goats and [miniature] cattle; they traded furs, walrus-tusk ivory, live polar bears and other exotic Arctic goods with Europe" (Folger 2017). Today, one of the best-preserved Norse ruins in Greenland is Hvalsey Church, located close to the modern-day settlement of Qaqortoq. During the Medieval Warm Period from about AD 900 to 1300, a relatively warm current flowing along the west coast of Greenland is believed to have provided fair conditions that allowed the settlers to maintain their Icelandic way of living. Yet between the thirteenth and fifteenth centuries, after almost five centuries of inhabiting the fjords of southern Greenland, the Greenland Vikings vanished (Nuttall 2017, 8). Several theories try to explain why this happened. One common explanation highlights a changing climate and the Vikings' inability to adapt as major factors in their disappearance (Diamond 2003). Additionally, a changing market economy and the devastation wrought by the Black Death in Europe, where the plague reached its nadir from 1347 to 1351, meant that the Vikings' lifeline to the "civilized" world was broken. As a result, "the Greenland Vikings were essentially victims of globalization and a pandemic" (Folger 2017)—presaging global events more than five hundred years later. Yet during the early stages of the COVID-19 pandemic, Greenland quickly emerged as one of the least scathed, leveraging its remoteness to quickly seal itself off from global aviation networks (Landslægeembedet 2021).

Intimate matrix

Around AD 1300–1400, small groups of Inuit hunting tribes from the Arctic shores of North America entered Greenland in the northwest, specifically in the Thule region (Taagholt 1991). The region's name comes from Greek and Latin, indicating the common practice of foreign names being used for Greenlandic places.

A traditional sealskin tent in Qaarusulik, 1936.

A traditional turf house in Kullorsuaq, 1936.

In ancient Greek and Roman literature, Thule is the farthest north. Ultima Thule represents a metaphorical place beyond "the borders of the known world" (Herrero 2015, 122). This name can be seen as a foreign/Western imposition not only on Greenland's toponymy but on its landscape and culture, too. The Thule Inuit called themselves Inuit, meaning "the people" (Grant 2010). By AD 1500, the Thule Inuit had spread almost entirely around Greenland, exploring and hunting its coasts and fjords (Gulløv 2004). In other words, they originated in Canada and entered Greenland in the northwest, eventually migrating further east and south. By the end of the eighteenth century, the "Little Ice Age"—which had initially started with a decrease in mean global temperatures around 1300—started drastically changing settlement patterns in Greenland. During this period of global cooling, population on the island's northern and northeastern coasts declined to practically zero (Lynnerup 2015). This highlights the outsized impact of climatic shifts on Greenlandic society given its rough terrain and latitudinal "extremeness." New population centers appeared on the west coast, which is the area where most of the present-day Greenlanders live. Today there is still a noticeable divide between west and east Greenland that cuts across social, economic, and linguistic lines.

In terms of habitation, in summer, the Thule Inuit occupied skin tents structurally supported by whale bones or driftwood. The skins were arranged with the hair side facing inward for better thermal insulation (Grønlands Nationalmuseum & Arkiv 2021). In winter, the Thule Inuit moved to semi-subterranean homes made of snow, stones, whalebones, and turf. *Igloos*—Inuit winter houses exclusively made of snow—were mainly used by hunters on long hunting expeditions rather than as permanent snow houses. Built as a shelter for the night or a couple of weeks, these dwellings were made of compacted snow cut into blocks with a large knife. These were placed on top of each other in a spiral course resulting in a dome-shaped structure (Mellor 1968, 3). Oftentimes, there were larger communal ensembles of Inuit winter houses (*igluvigaq*) with numerous circular structures joined together "in a long passage . . . so that one could go all over the place without exposure to the weather" (Rasmussen 1927). These joined-up structures helped reinforce social bonds, as did large communal turf houses (*ittilorat*, occupied until the 1920s) and the sharing of food, which continues to this day. Kinship and the collective remain central to Greenlanders' traditional relationship to the built environment and to the land itself.

In the past, the Inuit were semi-nomadic, and "seasonality shaped every aspect of traditional life" (Sheppard and White 2017, 27). Temporary settlements were linked to the migration routes of marine mammals such as whales, seals, porpoises, and walruses, which were hunted and used for "food, fuel, clothing, kayak skins, and tent material" (Grydehøj 2014, 209). For Inuit, both in the past and today, wayfinding and traveling through the landscape is more than just moving from point A to B: it is a way of being (Aporta 2004, 13). Moving is deeply embedded in Inuit culture, involving "a multisensory monitoring of one's surroundings" and various (often physical) ways of communicating about orientation, travel routes, and hunting grounds (Elixhauser 2018, 50). In this dynamic environment across which Inuit regularly travel and move, there are also moments to rest, pause, and reflect—for example, in the Inuit winter house. In both the Inuit architectural imagination and vocabulary, orientation inside the Inuit winter house (*igluvigaq*) is expressed similarly as orientation on the land. For example, in West Greenland, when going to the back of the house, one would say *kangi*-, "toward the interior of the land," and when going to the front, one would say *kimmut*-, "toward the sea" (Desrochers-Turgeon 2019). Such conceptualizations reveal the ways in which the built environment embodies experiences of moving across the Greenlandic landscape.

In addition to the multiple frames of reference of orientation, a strong storytelling tradition helps sustain a culture of traveling on the land, snow, and ice. The ability to communicate an in-depth

Ole Andreassen from the village of Ikerasak, western Greenland, shows his catch of the day—including fish and bird eggs—in a well-equipped kayak.

knowledge of routes and place names carries high social value and represents a source of personal pride (Aporta 2004, 32). The sharing of myths, proverbs, and tales that are connected to place names, topographic features, and encounters with people and animals has helped to develop a collective memory (Whitridge 2002). The interconnectedness of Greenland's natural and cultural landscapes produces a "memoryscape" (Nuttall 1992), resulting in "a simultaneously real and imaginary geography" (Rundstrom 1990). This collective memory and complex relation to the landscape is transmitted from one generation to the next. Anthropologist Tim Ingold and historian of science Michael Bravo have made similar observations relating to Greenland's memoryscape. Ingold's observations have helped elevate a "dwelling perspective, . . . in which the landscape is constituted as an enduring record of—and testimony to—the lives and works of past generations who have dwelt within it. In so doing, they have left there something of themselves" (Ingold 1993, 152). Bravo points out that within Inuit society exist an "intimate matrix of connections" and a "succession of shifting horizons . . . at once geographical and emotional" (Bravo 2019, 20). Within Inuit ethnography, this culturally complex and "historically sedimented" relationship is not solely confined to the land, for it also includes the sea and icescapes (Whitridge 2002). As a result, over time and with the changing seasons, ways of seeing, living, and navigating change accordingly. Today, Greenlandic settlements are still intensely connected to the sea and ice, affecting its past and present urban planning (see chapter 5).

Exploration and collaboration

Encounters and collaborations between foreign explorers and Inuit navigators, travelers, and mapmakers have added another layer of complexity to Greenlandic histories, memories, and landscapes. Well before any of these collaborations took place, Europeans had already begun imagining and drawing polar maps

South Greenland, 2022.

despite never having approached the North Pole (Bravo 2019). Sometime between 1420 and 1439, Danish geographer Claudius Clavus was one of the first to map parts of the Arctic and label Greenland (Sigurdsson 1984). Clavus's map was followed by Gerhard Mercator's 1595 map "Septentrionalium Terrarum descriptio," which depicted Greenland at a roughly correct size and location.

Although the Inuit were among the first people to explore and utilize the land, sea, and ice in and around Greenland in daily life, from the fourteenth century onward, northern European and North American explorers, whalers, and scientists dominated foreign exploration of the Arctic (Taagholt 1991). Later, in the sixteenth century, encounters between Western explorers and Inuit often proved troublesome, as illustrated by the hostilities between British explorer Sir Martin Frobisher (1535–1594) and Greenlandic Inuit (Loovers 2020). Beginning in the late 1700s, however, European whalers sought to establish more amicable relations with coastal Indigenous peoples in the Arctic to support the trade of goods. Explorer John Ross (1777–1865) was one of the first naval officers to pursue this approach and emphasized collaborative relationships without using force (Loovers 2020). Many of those partnerships are included in original travel reports, such as the contributions of local Inuit Hans Hendrik (1834–1889), who played an important supporting role in several Arctic expeditions, or John Sakeouse (1797–1819), who assisted Ross. The Second Thule Expedition (1916–1918) which set out to map a little-known area of Greenland's north coast, was led by Knud Rasmussen with support provided by a Greenlandic Inuit man named Inûkitsoq. At least one expedition, the Fifth Thule Expedition (1921–1924), was assisted by an Inuit woman, Arnarulunguaq. Integral to the success of all these Arctic voyages were the experiences, communication skills, and maps of local Inuit hunters, storytellers, and interpreters. Foreign explorers became deeply fascinated by Indigenous mapmaking, even though Inuit were largely concerned with the "act of mapping," as opposed to the final product

A boat in the waters surrounding Kulusuk island, 2017.

(Rundstrom 1990). While mapmaking was a product of power and a tool for colonization, with foreigners instrumentalizing Inuit knowledge in order to navigate Greenland's extreme landscapes more safely, the practice also occasionally helped forge collaboration and companionship between foreign explorers and local Inuit.

One encounter involved Danish naval officer and Arctic explorer Gustav Holm (1849–1940) and the Inuit (Tunumiit) of the Ammassalik coast of eastern Greenland. After many failed attempts to reach Ammassalik, Holm succeeded in 1884 with the assistance of several Inuit men and women from South Greenland, including Hanseeraq as an interpreter, and a few Danish men (Grønlands Nationalmuseum & Arkiv 2021). To support Holm's expedition, an East Greenlandic hunter named Kunit carved out prominent coastal features in pieces of driftwood, such as "fjords, islands, nunataks and glaciers" (Bagrow 1960, 27). In exchange for the maps and other traditional East Greenlandic art and handicrafts, Holm provided European ironware, fabric, tobacco, and more. Initially, the tactile wooden maps were under-

Knud Rasmussen and Inûkitsoq, Second Thule Expedition, 1916.

Arnarulunguaq, Fifth Thule Expedition, 1921.

stood to be instruments that were felt by hand as travelers moved along the rugged Greenlandic shores in an *umiak* (a type of open skin boat). Recent arguments, however, including the work of archaeologist Hans Harmsen, suggest that these handheld wooden devices may have been used primarily for storytelling rather than for navigating the icy and treacherous waters of east Greenland. In other words, the intriguing Ammassalik maps are now considered anomalies and not representative of common navigational practice among the Inuit. They do, however, have a significant historic importance recognized by, for example, graduate students at the University of Greenland (*Ilisimatusarfik*), who, in 2016, started building an online repository of 3D models of the Gustav Holm collection, called the Ersersaaneq project. *Ersersaaneq* is a Greenlandic word and can roughly be translated to "creating knowledge through images" (Buijs 2018). The students' aim was to make the materials accessible to all and demonstrate "that these materials are not only important to Greenlandic history but are also part of a larger global collection of indigenous world heritage" (Fleisher et al. 2018). As of 2021, there are seventeen 3D digital models of the Holm collection available online. Despite this limited number, their easy online access and usage can provide opportunities for continued (international) research and collaboration; increase the understanding of traditional (East) Greenlandic tools, culture, and people; and spur other heritage projects in Greenland and the Arctic at large. A greater knowledge of Greenlandic heritage might also positively influence cityscapes more responsive to the nation's complex cultural history.

Colonization and decolonization

When Danish colonization started in 1721, largely via the activities of Hans Egede, a Dano-Norwegian Lutheran missionary, the process drastically reshaped Inuit culture, threatening to divorce it from the landscape. Dramatic changes in settlement patterns were one result of colonialism (Sejersen 2007, 27). Namely, as trading posts and settlements were founded along Greenland's west coast, "Inuit themselves were encouraged by Danish traders and administrators to move around the fjords, islands, and skerries" (Nuttall 2017, 9). Danish colonists had ulterior motives, namely, to push the Inuit to explore for and exploit fish, specifically cod. Subsistence hunting was gradually replaced by export-focused industrial fishing (Billingsley 2020). Two hundred years of Denmark's isolationist policy and its strong control over trade transformed Greenland into a productive and lucrative Arctic territory for itself (Nuttall 2017, 10). Early trading posts such as Godthåb (present-day Nuuk) became influential economic hubs still active and thriving today. In general, the creation of Danish-initiated trading posts and settlements led to the centralization of economic activity and population that is in fact being exacerbated today, leading to the depopulation of smaller villages. This Danish colonial approach demonstrates that urbanization in Greenland has been largely a foreign process difficult to map on preexisting more semi-nomadic and communal ways of living.

After World War II, Denmark ended its isolationist policy. While still administering Greenland as a colony for a few more years, until 1953, Copenhagen shifted its priorities to social welfare and infrastructural change as part of an effort to "modernize" (or, more precisely, "Westernize") both the country and Inuit society (Nuttall 2017, 10). The colonial Danish government translated this commitment in its G-50 policy, which was established in 1950 and implemented by the Greenland Commission and later taken over by the so-called Greenland Technical Organization (GTO). The GTO exacerbated and formalized the colonial process of breaking Greenlandic traditions by further forcing Inuit people to abandon their culture and permanently settle in so-called modern accommodations. They envisioned constructing six thousand new houses to replace the entirety of Greenland's collection of accommodations (Hemmersam 2021, 130). By urbanizing Inuit society, Denmark wanted to "improve" conditions in Greenland (Sejersen 2007, 27). This commitment was followed by the Danish G-60 policy, which aimed to concentrate economic development in the capital of Nuuk (at the time still named Godthåb) and the towns of Paamiut, Sisimiut, and Maniitsoq. Modernization efforts initiated by the G-50 and G-60 policies depended on Danish government subsidies, which increased exponentially (from DKK 28 million to DKK 109 million annually) between 1950 and 1962 (Nielsen 2016, 55). Money was flowing to Greenland, but the voices of its people were ignored. Up until the 1970s, the organization's personnel was entirely Danish. Few efforts were made to educate and train a local Greenlandic and skilled workforce (Hemmersam 2021, 130). Most Danish specialists and skilled workers lived temporarily in Greenland during periods of construction. However, excluding Inuit people from policymaking spurred numerous urban and social problems (as elaborated on in chapter 3). Moreover, changes in traditional lifestyles led to decreases in fishing and hunting opportunities, increased rates of unemployment, and psychological stress. These detrimental effects have contributed to elevated rates of alcoholism and domestic abuse and overall poor health outcomes (Bjerregaard 2020). While colonization de-

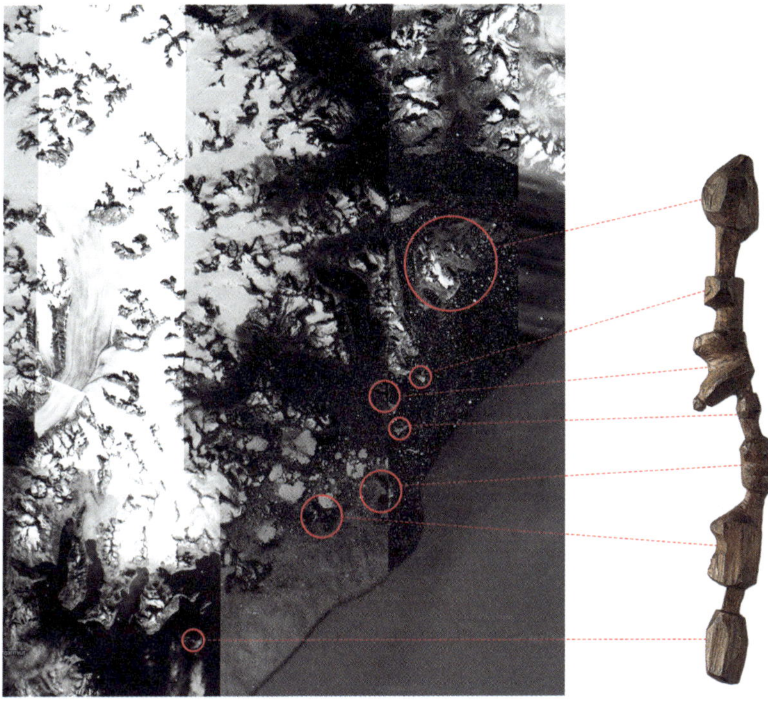

One of the Ammassalik maps from the 1880s in relation to contemporary satellite imagery.

livered certain advantages to Greenland (i.e., modern amenities and infrastructure), it also traumatized and scarred the people and their lands, sea, and ice.

During the postcolonial era of the 1950s, '60s, and '70s—a period sometimes referred to as "disguised colonialism" (Hansen 2021)—Greenland's primary industry, fishing, aligned with the GTO's proposed list of towns for economic concentration: Nuuk, Paamiut, Sisimiut, and Maniitsoq. However, the fixing of populations and infrastructure in specific locations made it difficult for the traditionally semi-nomadic Inuit to adapt to changes in food availability. One example of this is West Greenland's transi-

Danish-designed prefab houses in Nuuk, 1961.
© SABAM Belgium 2021.

tion from cod fishing to shrimp fishing (ca. 1960–1990) due to the decline in cod stock. The commercial collapse of the cod fishery industry in West Greenland was ultimately a "resource depletion" that resulted in the "urban decline" of many important fishing towns, such as Maniitsoq (Laruelle 2019, 7).

In the postwar period, Greenland experienced not only shifts to its urban form and economic activities but also its political arrangements with Denmark. In 1953 the long process of Greenland's decolonization commenced when Denmark voted to change the Danish constitution and integrate the island as a county in the Kingdom of Denmark, which was followed by the United Nations' recognition of Greenland's new status in 1954 (Olesen 2019). In 1979, as decided by public referendum, Home Rule was implemented in Greenland, followed in 2009 by another referendum in favor of Self Rule. The Home Rule Act was the first major stepping-stone for the people of Greenland, as they now had the right to elect their own parliament and government (Government of Greenland 2020). After a dispute over fishing rights with Brussels, Greenland initiated a public referendum in 1982 and left the European Union in 1985. The Greenland Treaty of 1985 formalized this so-called Grøxit (De Gruyter 2020). Today, Greenland has become a (post)-colonial territory amidst a still-ongoing decolonization that may eventually result in full independence from the Kingdom of Denmark (Carruth 2016).

Despite decolonization, Greenland's settlement pattern is largely centered on the economic hubs engineered by Danish colonization. Since Godthåb (present-day Nuuk) was the seat of government for the Danish colony of South Greenland, it had the necessary infrastructural and administrative networks in place. As a result, Nuuk became the economic, political, and administrative heart of contemporary Greenland. As a former small fishing village, Nuuk emerged and transformed relatively fast into something resembling a European city with agglomeration tendencies. In 2020, eighteen thousand people were living in Nuuk, or more than 30 percent of the nation's population (Statistics Greenland 2020).

Since the country's population and economy are largely concentrated in Nuuk, the city has become a magnet of unusual proportions. To put this in perspective, in the United Kingdom—a country considered to be dominated by its capital—in 2019, "only" 13.8 percent of people lived in London. This highlights Nuuk's extremely disproportionate weight within Greenland's geography and demography. To support its outsized population, public housing in Nuuk has been and continues to be of major importance.

Sisimiut, West Greenland.

Paamiut, Southwest Greenland.

Over the years (and as highlighted in chapter 3), however, Danish-funded and -designed housing and infrastructure, which contributed heavily to transforming Nuuk into a Westernized city, has not come without its problems. Similar urban issues, albeit at a smaller scale, also appear in emerging small- to medium-sized towns, such as Sisimiut, Ilulissat, and Qaqortoq. Many of these may be poised to grow as new infrastructure like airports and roads are built and as the population of Greenland further concentrates in a few key settlements.

In the twentieth century, Greenland quickly went from being isolated under Danish control to becoming a "dynamic, modern society based on technological infrastructure, urban development, democratic governance, and international relations" (Nielsen 2016, 48). Today, strong political and economic ties continue to link the country to its former colonizer. For example, Denmark still controls the island's international trade, military, and foreign affairs. Copenhagen also still contributes two-thirds of Greenland's budget, making Greenland highly financially dependent. Furthermore, although Greenland's former prime minister, Kim Kielsen, as well as the new government coalition between Greenland's left-wing Inuit Ataqatigiit party (IA) and pro-independence party Naleraq, support full Greenlandic sovereignty, this objective is difficult to realize because not everyone agrees on this outcome, as this would mean losing the annual block grant from Denmark (Rasmussen 2018). Additionally, current prime minister Mute Egede (elected in April 2021) and his team are pushing for pro-environmental decisions and are signaling strong concerns about the impact of heavy industries such as mining. Some argue that ever since Danish colonization took hold, inevitably, "the future of Greenland . . . is a hybrid Greenlandic-Danish future" (Grydehøj 2014, 218). The two countries' close, if fraught, relationship will likely manifest in the urban landscape of Greenland for a long time to come, especially when Danish materials, engineers, and architects continue to shape and design the country's buildings, streets, and neighborhoods.

Qaqortoq, South Greenland.

Nuuk, West Greenland.

Maniitsoq, West Greenland.

University of Greenland (Ilisimatusarfik),
Nuuk, West Greenland.

Housing and Public Projects

As Greenland's capital and only city, Nuuk has played a prominent role in the history of urbanization and housing in Greenland—and the many social ills that have resulted from this process, which are exemplified by a range of historical and contemporary housing projects. As numerous issues persist, there is a need to critique what went wrong with past housing and other public projects in order to set the stage for contemporary proposals that integrate themselves into the surrounding landscape, emphasize a strong sense of community, and empower local people.

Block P

The GTO's forced relocation of Inuit into modern homes during the 1950s and '60s (see chapter 2) is exemplified by Nuuk's infamous Block P. In a move away from the traditional single-family house, the two-hundred-meter-long, five-story concrete building testified to the failure of Danish housing policy in the 1960s. At one time, the country's largest modernist housing block was occupied by 1 percent of Greenland's population. This was a jarring shift, as decades prior most Inuit had been semi-nomadic. With its hallways "too narrow for people wearing heavy outdoor clothes" and lacking room for dogs or dogsleds (Vindum and Täckman 2012), Block P was entirely unsuitable for traditional Inuit lifestyles, as were other housing blocks built during this time. Since it was not designed for the Greenlandic context, many residents found it difficult to adapt, resulting in significant personal and social costs (Nordatlantens Brygge, 2013). Journalist Philip Lauritzen critically concluded, "Although [Block P] provided toilets and running water for everyone, [it] soon became an architecturally designed bomb of social maladjustment" (Vindum and Täckman 2012).

Block P, Nuuk, 1967.

Others, namely those involved in Block P's administration, viewed the housing complex more sympathetically. In 2012, Else Løvstrøm, communications officer of Block P's management association, offered, "Block P contains all good and all bad. Many have lived harmonious lives in that building, really good lives, but others have had a really hard time. It is very mixed" (Nielsen 2016, 48). In response to unfavorable public opinion toward Block P (and high maintenance costs), the Greenlandic Home Rule and Nuuk City Council decided in 2010 to demolish the building, which occurred two years later.

Prior to demolition of Block P and in a symbolic act to signal change, on Greenland's national day (June 21, 2009), artist Julie Edel Hardenberg attached an enormous Greenlandic flag to one side of Block P, made out of pieces of fabric donated by its inhabitants. After the building's demolition, residents were offered housing in the city's Qinngorput district (Sermitsiaq 2010). Yet this relocation came with its own issues: since the new housing is located in the shadow of the Ukusissat mountain, "half of the almost 1,000 residents [are] denied sunshine and warmth during the winter months" (Sørensen and Willumsen 2013, 186). In addition, local newspapers at the time reported that many people were unwilling to move to the new district due to potentially higher rent and the risk of becoming detached from the community (KNR 2010). Effectively, former Block P residents had little to no involvement in the design process of the new housing at Qinngorput.

In contrast, Block P residents were involved in the design process of a new strategic master plan for the site of Block P in combination with its adjacent neighborhood, Tuujuk (Uhre and Dahl 2017, 188). The Tuujuk neighborhood comprised several smaller housing blocks built in the early 1960s. Commissioned by Sermersooq Municipality (with Nuuk as its central city) and the government of Greenland, this project was called Nunarsuup Qeqqani Nuup Qeccani (NQNQ for short, or "In the Middle of the World, in the Middle of Nuuk"). The project's advisers comprised a group of design offices from Norway, the UK, and Greenland: Dahl & Uhre Arkitekter (Tromsø), TNT Nuuk (Nuuk), Asplan Viak landscape (Oslo), MDH Arkitekter (Oslo), Fantastic Norway (Oslo), 42 Architects + Regional Associates (London), and M:ARC and Arkitekti (Nuuk). When working with a large number of design offices and local residents, a dialogue-oriented design process is vital. In the NQNQ project, this is exemplified in the many conversations and workshops with locals that "informed and shaped the design of the spatial structure of the strategy plan, which in turn informed further dialogues" (Uhre and Dahl 2017, 174). This process of "oral knowledge exchange" also sought to integrate and effectively put to work the strong tradition of storytelling in Inuit culture (Uhre and Dahl 2017, 182). These discussions and mapping exercises led the project to increasingly revolve around a historic Arctic wetland on Block P's grounds, which helped provide an avenue for imagining a reorganized urban pattern for Nuuk (Uhre and Dahl 2017, 186). This reintroduced Arctic wetland would be tied into Nuuk's existing open surface water system and the city's

Project: In the Middle of the World, in the Middle of Nuuk (NQNQ).

ecological network. Furthermore, vital citywide upgrades would be needed to accompany new housing with comfortable and coherent streetscapes, shelter from the wind, connections to informal pathways, and places to sit and play. Overall, the team of designers' proposal, which encompassed a total area of 52,000 m^2, including space for three hundred homes, several new shops and businesses, a museum, and more, demonstrates the importance of international collaboration, a careful reading of the landscape, and a participatory approach.

Guest and experimental architectural offices also tried to address some of the site's social issues through their design projects. For example, the Norwegian architecture office Fantastic Norway proposed the House of Families, in which disadvantaged and single-parent families could find a welcoming group of people within Nuuk's wider community. Fantastic Norway's design

Street art in Nuuk, 2021.

envisioned small clusters of houses that are interconnected by "communal living areas, playrooms, kitchens and meeting places" (Warmann 2010)—potentially inspired by the communal ways of living of the (Thule) Inuit—and in doing so, creating safe spaces to meet and built new social connections. This concept also followed the office's ideology of an architectural practice that should push for "inclusive and socially aware" projects (Aasarød and Haffner, n.d.). This way of designing, as well as the large number of Norwegian architecture offices within the NQNQ project, also highlights Norway's close ties with Greenland and a shared understanding of spatial challenges in an Arctic context. Moreover, in terms of planning principles, there seems to be more cultural affinity between the two countries than between Greenland and Denmark, as a Danish employee of the Greenlandic government and a Greenlandic female professor also emphasized during an interview. Among many other reasons, Norwegian planners know what it means "to plan for and deal with vast landscapes that are sparsely inhabited" (Hansen and Løvstrøm 2021). In the past, the Greenland Commission and GTO acknowledged this as well and based some of their efforts on the "Norwegian post-war urban reconstruction" program (Hemmersam 2021, 133).

Although the collection of international teams conducted a careful reading of the project's relation to its surroundings, namely in terms of the ecological, social, and micro-climatical context, implementation of their ideas was on hold for a long time. Now, almost ten years after Block P's demolition, the Sermersooq Municipality has largely abandoned the rich and strong proposals developed during the NQNQ project, even though it initially commissioned and supported them. In part, the political willpower and financial capacity necessary to advance this large project was lacking. Many aspects of the project—often in a different size, density, or architectural form—did, however, inspire and shape various strategy, design, and regulation plans concerning Nuuk's current urban landscape (Sværd 2021). In addition to holding on to some proposed axial lines and blue-green infrastruc-

Qinngorput, Nuuk, 2021.

Construction of Atuarfik Narsasuaq – The School on the Plateau.

tures, the project's intention of providing spaces fostering social connections, storytelling, and knowledge exchange located in the heart of Nuuk paved the way for the 2019 design competition for a smaller area of the site, called Atuarfik Narsasuaq—The School on the Plateau. This competition was won by Copenhagen-based KHR Architecture and supported by ISTAK (contractor), Verkis (engineer), and VEGA Landskab (landscape architect). As in the aforementioned House of Families by Fantastic Norway, KHR envisions a cluster of seven interconnected buildings open to the public (Nordatlantisk Byggeri 2018), which "function as a gathering space for the whole town outside of school hours" (KHR 2020). Led by publicly owned development company Nuuk City Development A/S, the 17,000 m^2 centrally located new school would provide space for 1,200 pupils and, if all goes to plan, will be finished in 2023. This project will have a significant and positive impact on the educational landscape and social network of Nuuk. In addition to this school, in 2019, approximately 150 new apartments were completed at the Block P/Tuujuk site (Planstrategie 2019, 15). This is, however, fewer than the initial three hundred homes proposed as part of the NQNQ project. Also, it is still far from enough to alleviate the current severe accommodation shortage in Nuuk—a city that is "expected to grow considerably" in the near future (Peschardt, n.d.).

Housing and mobilities

In recent years, the city of Nuuk has tried to anticipate and react to its housing shortage by initiating a couple of large-scale contemporary and sustainable housing projects. Most of these new projects are located relatively far from the city center, however, making them inconvenient for many residents and arguably limited to people with relatively high income. One recent example is the ongoing project to build a new urban district within Nuuk called Siorarsiorfik. Organized by the local Sermersooq Municipality, this project originated from an international design competition in 2017, which was won by the Oslo-based Nordic Office for Architecture. Siorarsiorfik's large-scale and long-term planning project includes 3,400 new homes, several new schools, cultural facilities, and commercial areas, making it Greenland's largest urban development project (Nuuk City Development A/S 2018). Overall, the design proposal emphasizes a strong sense of community and is in dialogue with its surroundings. The Nordic Office for Architecture's proposal also demonstrates a solid understanding of microclimates in an Arctic context, light conditions, and topography, and generally promotes architectural solutions that foster local economic growth. Yet proposed districts such as this—similar to the new Qinngorput district—can exacerbate Nuuk's scattered urbanization and spatial fragmentation. With the new district cut off from Nuuk's city center by ridges, rocky hills, and rugged shorelines, Siorarsiorfik's residents would inevitably have to rely heavily on automobile transport (Grydehøj 2014). In addition to the Siorarsiorfik district, future urban expansion is expected to happen on the islands along Nuuk's coast (Sværd 2021). Thus water taxis may become a critical aspect of Nuuk's public transport network (Sværd 2021). In general, the limits to the built environment (i.e., lack of housing, topography, etc.) and their historical background (i.e., GTO) challenge the viability of new urban development projects and, at the same time, (when affordable) underscore the growing need for such new projects.

Additionally, the tight housing market in Nuuk and Greenland's other large settlements makes it difficult for young Greenlanders living or studying abroad to return home. One Greenlandic interviewee offered, "If people can't find a house in Greenland, they often choose to either stay in Denmark or move to Canada—which is very unfortunate" (Løvstrøm 2021). Limits to Greenland's accommodation infrastructure, especially in Nuuk, constrain local mobilities both literally and metaphorically, with young people unable to "move up" to purchase a home for a growing family, for instance. This lack of housing also results in the out-migration of people from Greenland. Related to this, a Greenlandic artist living temporarily in Copenhagen argued, “Foreigners who want to work in Nuuk oftentimes get offered housing, but for local Greenlanders that option is rarely available—which means that locals more often have to move away.” Privileging certain workers and certain jobs for housing tends to resemble historically narrow-minded examples “in that it continues to be the Greenlandic elites (the politicians and business leaders) and the international contractors (primarily the extractive industries) that are privileged to engage in the collective enterprise of imagining, deciding upon, and gradually [actualizing] Greenland’s future” (Tejsner 2017, 215).

Collaboration and cultural sensitivity

In addition to the Greenlandic elites and international contractors, foreign design firms also play a significant role in imagining the Greenlandic built environment. As evinced by Block P’s (unbuilt) strategic master plan as well as the more recent Siorarsiorfik and Atuarfik Narsasuaq project, the Sermersooq Municipality (with Nuuk as its central city) relies upon international design competitions for local neighborhoods, with a tendency to attract foreign, and specifically Scandinavian, design firms. In no small part, this reflects the lack of local offices that might be able to take the lead and push for Indigenous-led projects that are sensitive to local cultural and environmental needs. In 2013, for instance, only one Greenlandic person was studying architecture (Hersher 2016). Since Greenland still has very few local architects today (Løvstrøm 2021), only a small number of local residents possess the architectural skill set to lead larger design projects. In addition to Danish people leading Nuuk’s planning department, the paucity of Greenlandic architects leads to a preponderance of foreign design firms. Although foreign designers should be careful not to romanticize collaboration (Foster and Iaione 2016, 331), a strong participatory approach involving local people throughout the building design process is crucial, both to produce successful projects supported by the community and to train local architects. To achieve both objectives and to engage more deeply with the Greenlandic context, designing truly collaborative processes—with a particular focus on "those most vulnerable to being excluded from decision making" (Foster and Iaione 2016, 331)—is an important foundation for any design project.

Since the 1990s, Greenland has become a popular testing ground for internationally acclaimed architecture offices to explore cutting-edge designs in a remote landscape. Nevertheless, collaborating with residents and adapting one's design to the local environmental and cultural context are often missing elements, as demonstrated in the Nuuk Center (2005–2012), comprising a shopping mall and the administrative center for the new Greenlandic self-government. Compared to the adjacent Katuaq Cultural Center—constructed from 1994 to 1997, and (according to foreign standards) one of Nuuk's most architecturally noteworthy buildings, inspired by the northern lights and Greenland's mountains—the Nuuk Center lacks any significant reference or connection to its surroundings, both metaphorically and literally. Even though the Nuuk Center is considered a "symbol of the emerging state" (Hemmersam 2021, 146), this multistory building turned out to be more appropriate for European cities. If the building is an architectural expression of where the Greenlandic self-government is headed within its nation-building project, it is arguably embracing external, more than internal, ways of seeing Greenland (see chapters 4 and 5). Furthermore, being a center both of commerce and administration in the heart of Nuuk, this building can be considered an important node within the social and infrastructural network of Nuuk. Thus the designers had a responsibility to adhere to the surrounding urban landscape. With the potential to serve as a positive example, the building would have benefited from being more spatially and culturally sensitive.

In contrast, the Katuaq Cultural Center emphasizes local Greenlandic influences within a contemporary and international design disci-

Katuaq Cultural Center, Nuuk.

pline. Designed by SHL Architects—based in Copenhagen, Aarhus, and Shanghai—the building is inspired by Greenland's dramatic scenery and dancing night skies. In collaboration with local Greenlandic artist Buuti Pedersen, the building offers an expressive, light, and flexible space for people to meet and enjoy Greenland's vibrant cultural scene.

Another example is the winning yet still unrealized proposal for the new National Gallery of Greenland by Copenhagen and New York–based design firm Bjarke Ingels Group, designed in collaboration with local architecture offices TNT Nuuk, Ramboll Nuuk, and Inge Bisgaard of Arkitekti. By combining historical and contemporary Greenlandic art, standing in between traditional and modern Greenlandic identities, and benefiting from a site poised between the land and the sea, at the water's edge, the gallery straddles temporal, cultural, and geographic boundaries. The building's circular shape follows the terrain's topography, creating "a unique hybrid between the abstract shape and the specific

Katuaq Cultural Center, Nuuk, 2007.

location" (Ingels 2011). This architectural gesture and the collaborative nature of the project invite a diverse range of activities and tie the National Gallery strongly into the cityscape of Nuuk while embracing and enfolding the country's layered identities within one space.

Memory and data

To better accommodate Greenland's residents, the Greenlandic geodata portal NunaGIS may potentially serve as a pivotal element in the planning process of future design projects. Digital maps and geodata are increasingly becoming "fundamental tools" for Greenlandic municipalities and spatial designers (National Strategy of Geodata 2018, 55). Although digital data collection in Greenland is in its early stages (Sværd 2021), its output is gradually replacing Greenlandic maps based on aerial photography. These aerial photographs were mainly from the 1970s and 1980s and were simply too imprecise and "not worthwhile to use for planning" (Andersen 2018). Contemporary Greenlandic maps and plans increasingly rely on the Greenlandic geodata portal, NunaGIS, which aims to collect, translate, and symbolize complex data into clear, visual communication. Established between 2007 and 2012, this digital atlas covers Greenland at the national scale, provides accurate city maps, and displays geographical information such as vegetation zones, bird colonies, mineral/petroleum licenses, GPS-monitored caribous, hunting districts, historic buildings, territorial boundaries, and more. In recent years, much work has been done to upgrade this information portal, its website's performance, and its capacity to export the maps to a geospatial vector data format (shapefile). However, because this platform is and will be extensively used by architects and urban planners, a constant upgrade of and investment in NunaGIS—including adding new data layers touching upon local people's cultural knowledge and day-to-day needs—is vital to see impactful and positive results on the ground. One of these new layers can,

The Nuuk Center, 2015.

for example, refer to aspects of Greenland's "memoryscapes" (Nuttall 2009) by reflecting the strong interconnectedness of its natural and cultural landscapes (see chapter 2).

Greenland's evolving political landscape, as well as the rapidly changing climatic, economic, and technological contexts, may result in a multitude of new collective memories, infrastructures, and urbanization processes. When overlaid with local notions of living, human agency, and climate adaptive strategies, they can potentially serve as the blueprint of new "memoryscapes" anchored within changing socio-ecological contexts—revealing and catalyzing new spatial and social relationships. Incorporating this logic in geodata portals such as NunaGIS can potentially counter mid-twentieth century centralization efforts by Denmark in Greenland and realign centers of growth to better match local needs. Furthermore, and following recent scholarly work calling for infrastructure in Greenland that is "more culturally adoptable and adaptable; revealing, blurring, and reconnecting production and consumption" (Carruth 2016, 78), incorporating "memoryscapes" into urban planning can help ensure development that is connected to local resources and economic/commercial structures. Moving away from Danish/European-influenced ways of urbanization can generate settlement patterns more responsive to Greenland, its people, and its landscapes. Conclusively, since the meaning that humans attach to things is continually in flux, fluid, and malleable (Simonetti and Ingold 2018, 20), the idea of Greenland and its urban landscapes can be changed for the better—ideally by the people living there today rather than by outsiders.

Chromatic Geographies and Material Economies

Greenland's contemporary housing problems have multiple historical roots that involve not only the imposition of urban planning from the outside, but aesthetics and categorization schemes, too. In the 1950s and '60s, the work of Danish architects such as Viggo Møller-Jensen and Tyge Arnfred contributed heavily to colorful prefab housing typologies in Greenland (Vindum and Täckman 2012). In addition to the use of foreign building materials, the houses' chromatic geography—a term coined by landscape architect Gareth Doherty in referring to a color scheme or color code—represented a Danish colonial approach to codifying and controlling Greenland's resources and urban landscapes. Materiality and color provide lenses for understanding both the history of their use and the potential for their application in a more positive, bottom-up manner.

Prefabrication and building materials

Under Danish colonialism in Greenland, colors were painted on specific types of buildings, typically Danish-designed and Danish-financed prefab houses. In the early 1950s, over forty different housing types were eligible to be built with Danish financial support. Differences in standard housing types were linked to their purpose and sometimes their locality. In most cases, they lacked any modern amenities (i.e., running water and sewage treatment) (Hemmersam 2021, 130). Houses were relatively far apart to reduce the risk of fires spreading. In 1955, for easier production and assembly purposes, the forty housing types were reduced to approximately eight and further standardized (Bjarløv and Vladykova 2011, 1526). These newer models includ-

Red house in Kulusuk village, 2017.

ed "modern" kitchens and toilets. The types differed in size from 35m^2 to 120m^2 and were inconsistently numbered as followed: 1, 2, 3, 5, 10, 16, 17, and 25. In the 1960s, type 18D, 67/8, 67/12, 67/14, and 67/16 were added to the list. Throughout the 1970s, '80s, and '90s, these housing typologies were updated under the name of "Illorput"—for example, Illorput 43 and Illorput 82 (Bjarløv and Vladykova 2011, 1526). In 1998, the latest series, called Illorput 2000, was introduced. This series facilitated a more efficient use of insulation, often incorporated concrete and steel, and had a longer service life, among other improvements. A significant proportion of the Greenlandic population still lives in Illorput-type houses.

In the many housing variations, timber was an essential building material. Due to a lack of usable timber in Greenland, the prefabricated housing kits had to be shipped from Denmark to Greenland (Vindum and Täckman 2012, 47; Dzik 2015). Going back in time, the lack of native Greenlandic timber was already apparent during the time of the Greenlandic Vikings. In addition to visiting what they called "Stone-Slab Land" (present-day Baffin Island, Canada) (Kristjánsson 2005, 19) and "Vinland" (present-day Newfoundland, Canada) (Kristjánsson 2005, 25), they had to sail to "Markland" (present-day Labrador, Canada) to collect wood (Charpentier Ljungqvist 2005, 49). In other words, the Greenlandic Vikings relied upon their Norse traditions and used materials with which they were familiar rather than adapt and use locally available materials.

Greenland's built environment still relies heavily on the outside world for building materials. Climate change, however, may make certain materials more readily available, or even growable in Greenland itself. Warming temperatures, for instance, could make forestry both environmentally and economically viable in southern Greenland, and help the country become less dependent on imported wood. The Greenlandic Arboretum in Narsarsuaq, located in southern Greenland, has been collecting and experimenting with trees from the Alpine and Arctic tree line regions (Climate Greenland, n.d.). Besides this unique arboretum, however, other forest plantations are rare. The forest of the Qinngua valley, South Greenland—the most well known natural forest in Greenland, initially protected by law in 1930 by the Danish Colonial Administration (Høegh and Jacobson 2021)—could also inform future forestry management in the country. The north-south orientation of the fjord, the considerable distance to the sea and icesheet, and the surrounding mountains blocking cold winds, produce a beneficial microclimate for downy birches (*Betula pubescens*), gray-leaf willows (*Salix glauca*), and Greenlandic mountain ash (*Sorbus groenlandica*) (Edwards et al. 2010). Since these are mostly softwoods, which are often used to make doors, furniture, and window frames, Greenland would require hardwood species as well to allow for reliable and locally sourced wood construction. Due to the remoteness of Greenland and its distance from "forested neighbors," any potential future tree species will most likely be introduced by humans resulting in a "constructed ecosystem—a designed landscape" (Billingsley 2020). In this, sustainable forestry management will be crucial, as seen in neighboring Iceland. There, in the twentieth century, deforestation caused the birch (*Betula sp.)* woodland to go from covering approximately 15 to 40 percent of Icelandic land surface to less than 1 percent (Church et al. 2007). Climate change in Greenland may also cause other locally sourced materials to become more available. For example, the melting of the Greenlandic icebergs and glacial erosion creates massive amounts of sediment in the form of sand, gravel, mud, and rock flour. The first two commodities can be used for local urban expansion and infrastructural improvements (Bendixen et al. 2019), while these products of glacial erosion are valuable for global markets, too, mostly in the form of concrete. Local production of concrete is already happening in a limited capacity in, for example, the city of Nuuk.

The commercial viability of both Greenlandic timber and glacial sediment would change Greenland's relationship to the outside world—in terms of trade, economics, and more. In terms of design, it might also allow for a truly local, vernacular architecture based on Greenlandic building materials. Although experiments in this vein have so far been limited, seeing the rapid pace of change and high adaptive capacity in Greenland, Greenlanders might push for an accelerated and innovative creative design process in new building typologies. Furthermore, while the emerging material economies of timber, concrete, and more would be part of the global market, such enterprises, when owned locally, could ensure that power and control over Greenland's urban and material landscapes would be grounded in Greenland itself.

Color, power, and space

In addition to foreign materials, in the past, the Danish-designed and Danish-funded prefab buildings bore facades whose color indicated the building's function. The colorful categorization schemes in Greenland's built environment were, however, imposed by its colonizer, Denmark. Within Danish colonial design typologies, commercial and institutional buildings were red; hospitals were yellow; police stations were black; buildings related to communication infrastructure (such as telephone) were green; and fish-processing plants and infrastructure related to drinking water were blue (Dzik 2015). This approach provided a means of codifying and exercising control over Greenland's resources and urban landscapes. The linkage of color to function and land use reflected a material economy firmly anchored in natural resources located beneath the land, ice, or ocean surface. Colonial administrators also went beyond controlling the built environment. For instance, they introduced "color separations" to local Inuit clothing, especially women's attire (Hansen 2021). Some of the missionaries decided women had to wear a specific color to indicate, for example, if they were widowed or married, "and make it really visible on the street" (Hansen 2021). As in other colonial histories, color was thus linked to authority. In Greenland today, while some of the underlying functions indicated by the colors remain, the importance and underlying meaning of the colorful facades is shifting. For example, the public's attitudes of color increasingly reflect a touristic value, a comforting element, and more (Løvstrøm 2021). The choice of color is also often influenced by economics: as one Greenlandic academic said, "People sometimes paint their homes pink because it is the cheapest color on the market" (Løvstrøm 2021). It is important to note, however, that not all buildings in Greenland are colorful. Since the 1990s, and especially in Nuuk, the architectural trend of letting the building material's natural color "speak for itself" is growing. In other words, materials such as wood or concrete—while still mainly imported—are left "uncolored."

Yellow house in Uummannaq.

Blue house in Aasiaat.

Colorful Greenlandic houses in the town of Aasiaat.

Many recent architecture projects and proposals use this technique, such as the University of Greenland and Nuuk's Katuaq Cultural Center, and the proposed National Gallery of Art in Nuuk would, too.

In addition to "uncolored" facades, the perceived white color of snow and ice is also a large part of the Greenlandic urban landscape for a significant portion of the year. Especially in winter, the "absence" of color surrounding the settlements, towns, and cities is striking. The colorful Greenlandic houses stand in high contrast to the snowy landscape, making them even more visible than in summer. However, the "whiteness" (Bruun 2018) of snow is not as uniform as it seems. Although "snow reflects the entire spectrum of visible light, meaning it looks white to us" (Wills 2015), snow can have many colors as well. For example, when looking at long-lasting snowfields of several feet deep, one can find a palette of springtime blooms of algae ranging from yellow, green, orange, to

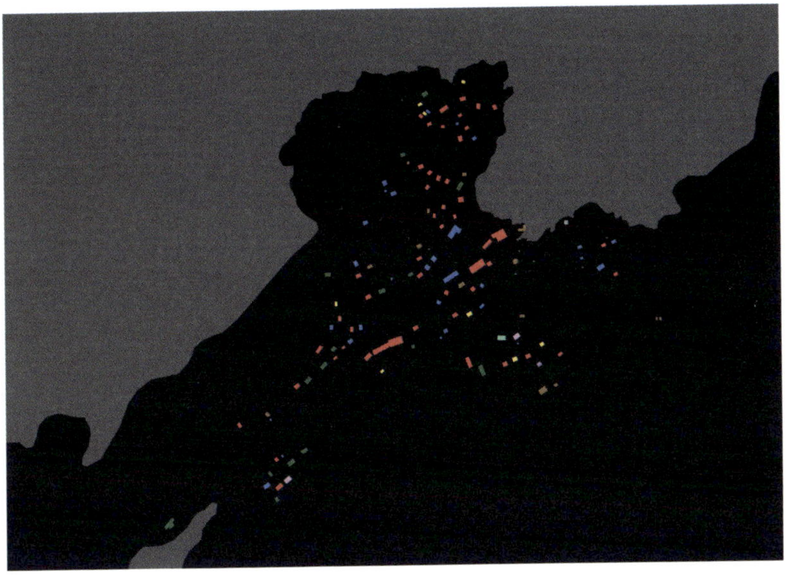

Color scheme of Kulusuk village, 2017.

red, reflecting a rich snow ecology (Milius 2000). The compression of old snow—the process responsible for glacier formation—can produce blue and sometimes blue-green ice (Peterson 1983). With a rapidly changing climate, snow and ice in Greenland's built environment might disappear and change the perception of and mobilities in those settlements. As further elaborated on in chapter 5, snow and ice are in fact an integral part of Greenland's urban landscape and support human life overall.

Looking beyond a building's individual color, materiality, and function, color can also take on a more abstract symbolic meaning in the urban landscape. Reimagining new color schemes, color codes, or chromatic geographies, and embracing new meanings, identities, and collective values can help create a unique urban landscape that empowers nation-building. Connecting aesthetics and politics, color can serve as a strong design element within specific programs, forms, and policies (Doherty 2010).

Color is not neutral. It can reinvent "the social collective of the city," in turn influencing the city's urban spaces and its people (Burdett and Kaasa 2010). As painter, photographer, and academic Lois Swirnoff puts it, "Instead of considering [the role of color] as embellishment, additive or extrinsic to urban patterns, color may be regarded as a special attribute of form itself, a shaping or *trans*forming component" (Swirnoff 2000). Any new coloration of Greenland's built environment should therefore involve local input, emotion, and creativity. These are aspects that may support a town's new visual signature, its efforts to be relevant and to generate a direct dialogue with and effective visual response to its history and potential alternative futures. Although Greenland's current chromatic geography mainly follows individual preferences and the market economy, color could become a "collective" and "vernacular expression" (Swirnoff 2000) that looks beyond capitalism, Greenland's resource imaginaries, and colonial history. Despite the colonial origins of colors schemes on buildings, colors can become even more central to Greenland's national identity and deliberately engage in outwardly representing and potentially even shaping its nation-building project.

In this light, Greenland's nation-building project should also be scrutinized. One could argue that nation-building itself is actually a capitalist endeavor aimed at accumulating revenue within the hands of those who control the state. In the end, this is a process that might not directly benefit local people or spaces used by local residents. With the national branding slogan "Pioneering Nation," the Greenlandic government seems to be embracing external, more than internal, ways of seeing the country. Greenland's national tourist board, Visit Greenland, which manages the country's perception, image, and brand, aims to appeal to adventure-seeking foreign tourists, demonstrating how nation-building is in many ways a marketing exercise (Thisted 2015). Reimagining new color schemes for Greenland's built environment can form a part of Greenland's outward-looking nation-building project if the colors represent and support local people, spaces, and policies.

Narsaq, 2022.

Aasiaat during the winter season.

13

Ittoqqortoormiit, formerly Scoresbysund.

Tasiilaq village.

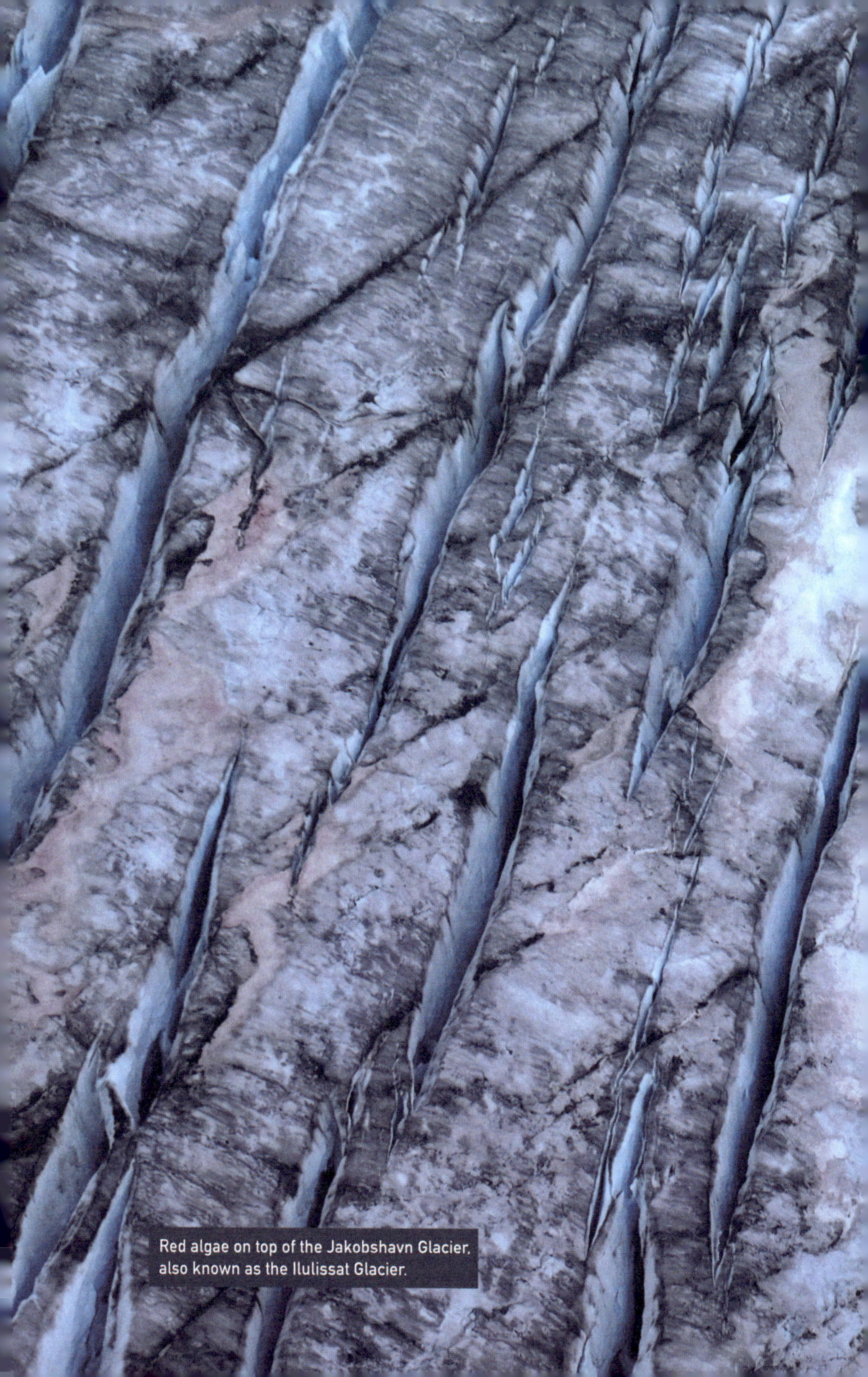

Red algae on top of the Jakobshavn Glacier, also known as the Ilulissat Glacier.

Arctic Tourism and Urban Growth

The ongoing airport expansion in Ilulissat, briefly discussed in the first chapter, offers a useful moment to examine the town's history and potential future growth patterns resulting from its new airport and the increasing numbers of tourists. As part of the ongoing reorganization of Greenland's aeroscape, significant improvements in airport infrastructure can strengthen an airport and town's pivotal position and create momentum across different infrastructural scales and urban spaces. In Ilulissat, this process of growth is also intertwined with its neighboring ice fjord, propelling the tourism industry in the city and the broader region.

UNESCO World Heritage

Ilulissat, which means "iceberg" in Greenlandic, is one of Greenland's leading tourist destinations thanks to its close proximity to the nearby ice fjord. The UNESCO World Heritage–listed Ilulissat Icefjord is located on the west coast of Greenland, about three hundred kilometers north of the Arctic Circle, and covers a large area where the Greenland Ice Sheet flows out to sea via the Jakobshavn tidewater glacier, known locally as Sermeq Kujalleq. Researchers have studied this large glacier for over 250 years, which has contributed to scientists' understanding of the world's rapidly changing climate (Bosson et al. 2019). Next to the forty-kilometer-long ice fjord sits Ilulissat, a scenic town of 4,670 people. Here, the almost continuous calving of the ice front, the icebergs' large size, and their proximity to the town create an urban landscape in which ice is distinctly front and center. However, the icebergs have long been seen by tourist organizations and foreign agencies as so sublime that their aesthetic value has been priv-

Ilulissat, 2021.

ileged over Ilulissat's urban landscape and local culture, leading tourists to expect an "untouched and human-free landscape" (Smed 2017). This perspective is also apparent in the World Heritage Committee's decision to inscribe the Ilulissat Icefjord on the World Heritage List. Published in 2004, the official justifications focus primarily on the "memorable natural spectacle" of the ice, the site's "relative ease of accessibility," and its importance for scientific research (World Heritage Committee 2004). UNESCO does recommend "tak[ing] into account the growing pressures from tourism," but does not directly refer to Ilulissat's urban landscape or culture (World Heritage Committee 2004). In other words, Ilulissat's local "culture is undermined as a value in itself" (Smed 2017). Problems with UNESCO World Heritage designations, especially in urban settings, have been raised in scholarly work before now. Among them are the difficulty of sustaining growth in a place that is meant to be conserved, and the challenge of maintaining locally produced notions of heritage, authenticity, and sense of place (Pendlebury et al. 2009). Since tourism is a "designated future key industry" for Greenland (Schrot et

Ilulissat harbor, 2021.

al. 2019), national tourist organizations such as Visit Greenland, as well as designers, can play an important role in promoting and translating Ilulissat's strong cultural and urban connection with the ice. Within this process, however, it is critical for designers to be aware of the risk of commodifying ice, imposing external values and valuations onto the ice, even when internal actors (such as Visit Greenland) adopt external values. As seen in the next sections, by looking beyond the site's "glaciological uniqueness" (Hunt 2014) for touristic purposes, one may find a deeper connection to the region's histories, cultures, and ecologies.

Ecosystem and product

The ice floe's connection to human settlement runs deep and can be traced back many centuries. For example, even before the establishment of Jakobshavn (now Ilulissat) as a Danish colony in 1741, there were many other settlements close by in the same region, including Sermermiut on the north side of the fjord and

Jakobshavn Glacier, Ilulissat, 2021.

Qajaa on the south side of the fjord. The name Sermermiut, which in Greenlandic means "the place of the glacier people," highlights residents' strong connection to their local glacier (GEUS, 2021). Sermermiut was inhabited by the Saqqaq, Dorset, and Thule people (Larsen and Meldgaard 1958) and was abandoned around 1850 "when glacier movement forced the inhabitants to Ilulissat or nearby villages" (Lindsey 2005, 934). Over time, various groups decided to settle next to the Jakobshavn glacier as a result of its rich and biodiverse ecosystem. The glacier's meltwater contains large quantities of nutrients and, because of the constant motion/turbulence of calving icebergs, warm and nutritious water can move up from the deeper layers to the surface (Ilulissat Icefjord Centre 2021). This generates massive amounts of plankton, attracting a wide range of crustaceans, fish, marine mammals, and birds. As a result, the ice facilitates rich hunting grounds, which in effect support human life in this extreme polar environment. Historically, rich hunting grounds have long served as a place for encounters with animals and possibly with other peoples, such as the Norse, although there is very limited recorded evidence of direct contact to support this claim (Sutherland 2000, 239). Today, the ice fjord's rich ecosystem remains essential for a large portion of the region's inhabitants and Ilulissat's fishing economy, which includes the largest shrimp-processing plant in northern Europe (Lindsey 2005, 934).

For polar communities, which traditionally depended fully on natural resources, tourism has lately become a potential means to diversify one's income (Smed 2014, 269). In 1991, tourism became part of Greenland's national development strategy (Kaae 2002). In the subsequent years, Ilulissat transformed into a polar tourism destination and became a part of the global tourism industry. The town is mostly dominated by European and North American visitors, with a recent noticeable increase in Asian tourists (Greenland Tourism Statistics 2019; Breum 2021). As in many other places around the world, however, Ilulissat's tourism industry was put on hold due to the COVID-19 pandemic. Many people working in tourism had to adapt and find a temporary occupation, such as local Inuit tour guide Jan who became a bus driver in Ilulissat. When restrictions on international air traffic are lifted, expectations are that tourism will continue to increase in the same upward trend as before the global pandemic. These tourists—due to the increased understanding and rate of climate change—will increasingly be part of a new stage of tourism: "last chance tourism" (Lemelin et al. 2010) or, some might even say, "dark tourism" (Stone and Sharpley 2008), where icebergs have become "spectacles" and "commodified products" (Lam and Tegelberg 2020, 148, 173). Last chance and dark tourism include places where tourists presumably go "before it is too late" (Smed 2014, 270). In the case of Ilulissat, this "place" refers specifically to its ice fjord and glacier, not necessarily to the town itself. The town of Ilulissat—which is experiencing a "rapid economic surge" (Hook 2019)—is, however, facilitating this "booming" tourism industry. At a larger scale, tourists' desire to visit the region before it is irrevocably changed may, however, exacerbate the physical and ecological changes in the Arctic region (Palma et al. 2019).

Jakobshavn Glacier, Ilulissat, 2021.

Icebergs in the waters surrounding Ilulissat, 2021.

Ilulissat Icefjord Centre

Just outside of Ilulissat lies the "Kangiata Illorsua—Ilulissat Icefjord Centre" designed by Danish architecture office Dorte Mandrup, which capitalizes on Sermeq Kujalleq's natural amenities. A minimalist 1:12 model was presented at the Venice Biennale of 2018, construction of the project started in 2019, and the Icefjord Centre opened its doors on the July 3, 2021. Constructed with imported Danish materials, the building is the first of six new visitor centers to be built in Greenland in support of "urban and tourist development" (Smárason 2021, 6). In addition to providing a high-quality exhibition and gathering place, according to the architects, the Icefjord Centre was designed to "blend in with the impressive landscape while offering local residents, tourists, and climate researchers the ultimate vantage point from which to absorb the historic atmosphere of the Icefjord" (Dorte Mandrup, n.d.). This idea follows the Western aesthetic tradition of providing viewpoints and framing the landscape (Urry 1992). Viewing platforms are mostly located on a high point in the landscape, privileging the "tourist gaze" (Urry, 1992). On the one hand, it is debatable whether most locals would choose to engage with the ice in this manner. If the design were to follow local perspectives on seeing and experiencing the ice, places as these would most likely be situated at a low point, close to the water, replicating how the ice would be seen from a kayak, *umiak*, or fishing boat. On the other hand, due to UNESCO zoning guidelines, difficult ground conditions, and the need to keep a safe distance from the shoreline (with its risks of tsunami-like waves due to the turning of icebergs), the decision, by the municipality and architect, of where to locate the Icefjord Centre was limited. The site of Ilulissat's former heliport, in between the town and the ice fjord, turned out to be the most practical location. The functionality of the former heliport, which has been inactive since 1984, has been adopted by the new Icefjord Centre in the sense that it is a hub connecting different paths of movement and groups of people. Helicopter activity has been relocated to Ilulissat's current airport, located on

Ilulissat Icefjord Centre, 2021.

the northern edge of town. Although the Ilulissat Icefjord Centre has opened only recently and has yet to experience large volumes of tourists, it promisingly serves as a bridge and catalyst between the town of Ilulissat and its ice fjord.

Tourism and growth

The relationship between Ilulissat and its ice fjord touches upon a significant topic in the field of Arctic tourism: the interplay between tourism and sustainable adaptation and growth of the respective impacted community (Kaján 2014). Owing to Ilulissat's limited accommodations for tourists, by the summer of 2016, the town had already reached its maximum capacity of approximately thirty thousand visitors (Visit Greenland 2017). Today, with the easing of restrictions on international air traffic (due to COVID-19), in addition to a long waiting list for housing, any increase in the number of tourists will require more places to stay. This foreseen development raises the need for the urban expansion of Ilulissat and a spatial analysis of how to carefully balance these demands. Since Ilulissat aims to be "the number one 'green' tourist destination in the Arctic," this will require "special emphasis on CO_2 neutrality, waste management, renewable energy, and energy-efficient solutions" (Ilulissat Steering Group 2018), as well as sustainable construction techniques and critical design proposals that incorporate the town's strong relation to the ice.

The assessment of sustainability, however, might differ in Greenland compared to countries where resources and transportation are abundant or nearby (Møller and Lading 2020). Also, since the Ilulissat ice fjord is a UNESCO World Heritage site, restrictions on expansion apply and are translated in a "landscape buffer zone" and "near-urban buffer zone" (Ilulissat Steering Group 2018). In addition to UNESCO's zoning guidelines restricting the southeast border of Ilulissat, the sea in the west and the town's water supply in the east (Jessen et al. 2014) make possibilities for urban expansion "very limited" (Ioannides 2019, 219) and possible only toward the north, further away from the ice fjord. This, however, might result in potentially disconnecting the town from the ice fjord, leading urban expansion to run close to Ilulissat's airport, which in itself comes with building restrictions. As signaled by several local interviewees, this situation could

Ilulissat, 2021.

lead to an increased densification of the built environment in Ilulissat. Besides spatial limitations, local people also challenge the viability of urban growth and expanding tourism in their town. Although Ilulissat residents are predominantly positive (92.4 percent) about tourists visiting their town (Visit Greenland 2019), they have become increasingly concerned by "the threat of being overrun by tourists"—"a challenge that will be even bigger once [Ilulissat's] new airport is completed" (Hook 2019). Some residents take an even more critical view. They argue that the new runway at Ilulissat Airport, which is expected to be finished by the end of 2023 (Kalaallit Airports 2020), could become "problematic in the near future as this could lead to the arrival of direct high-capacity flights" (Ioannides 2019, 219). Such flights may include many people who might be less "environmentally aware"—in contrast to "the tourists [they] receive now [who] more or less have some background knowledge before they arrive in Greenland" (Ioannides 2019, 219). One local Inuit guide mentioned that he would like Greenlandic flights, hotels, and tours to be even more expensive to limit the exponential growth of tourism. He expects there will come a point when the municipality will have to intervene and cap the number of visitors. Potentially, these limitations

and challenges—in addition to Ilulissat's strong "entrepreneurial milieu" (Baerenholdt 2000, 88)—could also catalyze opportunities to reimagine the relationship between Ilulissat's built and natural environment, as well as with tourism, culture, and the town's neighboring settlements. Yet local perspectives should be emphasized in any design project seeking to elevate urban experiences alongside and within the natural environment.

Overall, Ilulissat sits at the intersection of a vast network of people, distended global tourist networks, climate change science, rich ecosystems, hunting grounds, and more. In effect, constant change and movement in the landscape are integral to the region's inhabitants, identity, and cultural knowledge. In this highly dynamic environment, designers can help translate Ilulissat's complexity to tourists instead of designing commercial displays for easy consumption. At the city scale, continued and careful consideration of the relationship between nature, culture, and the built environment, anticipating and balancing the impacts of tourism and embracing Ilulissat's urban connection with the ice, can strengthen future decision-making and design processes.

Housing in Ilulissat, 2021.

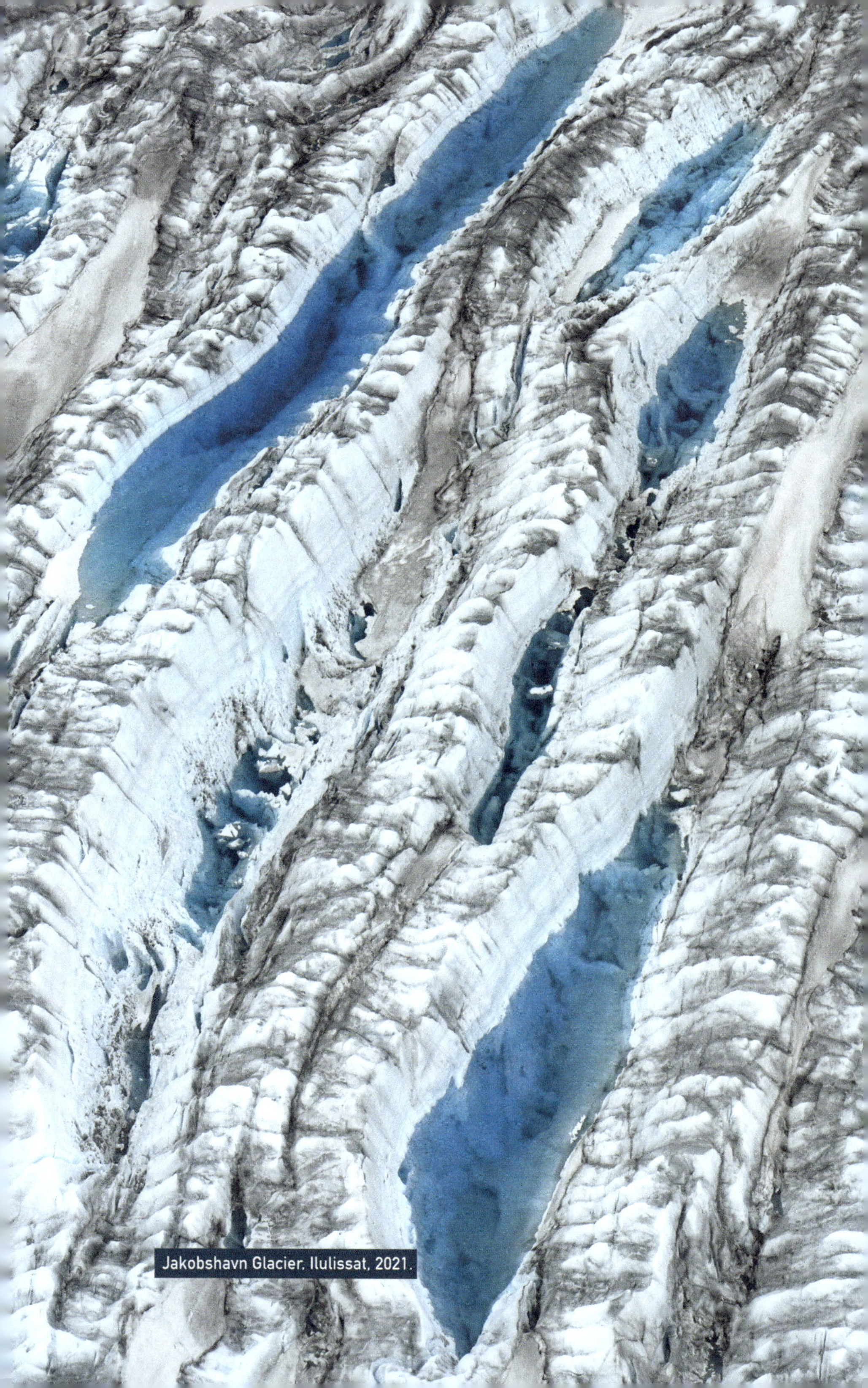

Jakobshavn Glacier, Ilulissat, 2021.

Conclusion

Urbanization in Greenland is a deeply layered and historically complex palimpsest ranging from the Greenlandic Vikings to a (post)colonial territory amidst still-ongoing decolonization. Over time, the ability to adapt to a changing climate, both environmentally and politically, has proven to be of central significance in the rise or fall of the people inhabiting Greenland's extreme landscape, among them the Greenlandic Vikings, who relied upon their Norse traditions and used materials with which they were familiar, rather than locally available materials. In contrast, the Thule Inuit—who are the ancestors of the present-day Inuit—developed an intimate matrix of connections between their culture and the local landscape, resulting in an architecture and lifestyle adapted to the seasons, the availability of food, and more. When Danish colonization began in 1721, the process drastically reshaped Inuit culture, threatening to divorce it from the landscape. In addition to the gradual replacement of subsistence hunting with export-focused industrial fishing, dramatic changes in settlement patterns were one result of colonialism (Sejersen 2007, 27). Danish colonists instrumentalized urbanization in Greenland as a means of imprinting their culture onto preexisting, more semi-nomadic and communal ways of living. Today, the two countries' close, if fraught, relationship will likely manifest across the urban landscape of Greenland for a long time to come, especially when Danish materials, engineers, and architects continue to shape and design Greenland's buildings, streets, and neighborhoods.

This is especially apparent in Nuuk. Greenland's capital tends to attract foreign, and specifically Scandinavian, design firms. In no small part, this reflects the lack of local offices that might be able to take the lead and push for Indigenous-led projects sensitive to local cultural and environmental needs. Since the 1990s, Greenland has also become a popular testing ground for internationally acclaimed architecture offices to explore cutting-edge designs in a remote and extreme landscape. Collaboration with residents and adapting one's design to the local context is, however, often missing. A strong participatory approach involving local people throughout the design process is crucial, both to produce successful projects supported by the community and to train local Greenlandic architects. Such a collaborative approach is exemplified in the "In the Middle of World, in the Middle of Nuuk" (NQNQ) project, which was led by a collection of foreign architecture offices. Although largely unbuilt, this work became influential for other planning and architecture proposals in central Nuuk.

More broadly, Greenland's urban identity has long been shaped by the outside. For example, in the past, color categorization schemes represented a Danish colonial approach to codifying and controlling Greenland's resources and urban landscapes. But today the use of color can be a powerful design tool, as it can represent a visual expression of the Greenlandic people, its spaces, and policies. Connecting aesthetics and politics through the use of color may also support a vernacular architecture that is locally grounded and embraces new meanings, identities, and collective values.

Another way to promote a vernacular Greenlandic architecture is to use locally available materials. In the past, the scarcity of wood as a building material influenced Greenlandic architecture during Danish colonialism. Today, Greenland's built environment still relies heavily on the outside world for building materials, although, due to a rapidly changing climate, new opportunities might arise. In terms of wood, if climate change were to make forestry both environmentally and economically viable in southern Greenland, the country could depend less on importing wood as a construction material. Moving away from Danish/European-influenced urbanization can support settlement patterns more responsive to Greenland, its people, and its landscapes.

In addition to the Danish colonialism, architects, and materials that have drastically reframed Greenland's built environment, the US military also had a large influence on Greenlandic communities and infrastructures, largely through the construction of

Greenland's "aeroscape." While Greenland's aviation infrastructure was initially designed to match American security needs, in its pursuit of greater independence from Denmark, the Greenland Self Government is both centralizing and globalizing its aeroscape. As it is streamlined to better align with the country's population centers, while also being reconfigured to attract global capital and tourists, the country's cozy airports where distant relatives are bound to run into one another may be replaced by slick, anonymous international airports—prototypical "non-places" (Augé 1995). The remaking of Greenland's aeroscape has implications not only for geopolitics and geoeconomics, but for the viability of local livelihoods and entire villages that have come to depend on airports built by the US military in the mid-twentieth century. One effect of Greenlandic self-rule may be the realignment of the country's aeroscape to support needs determined by the center of Greenlandic political and economic activity: Nuuk. As a result of this centralization, the economic and social underpinnings of settlements that became lively places both because of and despite American military interventions may disappear. While the "imperial debris" of bygone empires usually takes the form of crumbling ruins (Stoler 2008), vibrant places with their own histories and meanings can also endure. Postcolonial nation-building efforts that exclude post-imperial places from rationalized economic and political networks may cause their demise.

Certain casualties of Greenland's self-rule may be the infrastructure, livelihoods, and deep sense of place that have formed in villages whose original imperatives for existing—American military objectives—have long since dissipated. Several interviewees in Kulusuk made clear that they believe the government wishes people to move to Tasiilaq or even farther west. While the "everyday distributions and social life of infrastructure" (Anand et al. 2018, 13) command attention, the consequences of its redistribution and demise, or the afterlife of infrastructure, should, too. Across the Arctic and beyond, as Indigenous peoples gain sovereignty over their lands, they will undoubtedly build infrastructural networks more attuned to their needs than did the previous military or colonial powers. Accommodating the people "in between" who have been transforming colonial and imperial imprints on the landscape into their homes for hundreds of years, however, will require trade-offs in the Indigenous-led design of infrastructure, logistics, and nation-states.

Besides negatively impacting places such as Kulusuk village, changes in Greenland's aeroscape—such as the airport expansion at Ilulissat, for example—can strengthen an airport's pivotal role and create momentum across different infrastructural scales and urban spaces. In Ilulissat, this process of growth is also highly intertwined with its neighboring UNESCO World Heritage–listed ice fjord, which propels the local tourism industry. Since tourism is a "designated future key industry" for Greenland (Schrot et al. 2019), designers can help promote and translate Ilulissat's complex relation to the ice instead of designing commercial displays for easy consumption. In exploring different ways of looking beyond the site's "glaciological uniqueness" (Hunt 2014) for touristic purposes, one may find a deeper connection to the region's histories, cultures, and ecologies. At the city scale, balancing the impacts of tourism and elevating Ilulissat's urban connection with the ice can strengthen future decision-making and design processes and, ultimately, the people of Ilullisat.

Urbanization in Greenland is entangled in a wide range of historic processes, which were often beyond the control of the Greenlandic people. As urban conditions and futures are intimately bound to all life on the island, today Greenland has the choice to better design its cityscapes in relation to its local sociocultural and ecological context. On the one hand, these efforts are challenged by much uncertainty—such as natural processes taking place more quickly as a result of climate change (e.g., thawing permafrost). On the other hand, now is the time to further unpack the processes that have shaped the Greenlandic built environment and to engage in new ways of seeing and designing places, ways that promote inclusion, participation, and climate adaptation.

Bibliography

Aasarød, Håkon Matre, and Erlend Blakstad Haffner. n.d. "About—Fantastic Norway." https://www.fantasticnorway.no/?page_id=14.

Air Greenland. 2020. "Annual Report Air Greenland A/S 2020." Nuuk: Air Greenland. https://www.airgreenland.com/media/1538831/arsrapport-master_eng_web.pdf.

Anand, N., A. Gupta, and H. Appel. 2018. "Introduction: Temporality, Politics, and the Promise of Infrastructure." Pp. 1–40 in *The Promise of Infrastructure*. Chapel Hill: Duke University Press.

Andersen, A. 2016. "Greenland, My Greenland—Accessing Greenlandic History, Identity and Nation-Building through Its Nation-Branding Strategy, a Tourist Website and 247 Comments." In *Green Ice: Tourism Ecologies in the European High North*, edited by S. Abram and K. A. Lund. London: Palgrave Macmillan.

Andersen, Hanne Holm. 2018. "Planning and Construction." *National Strategy of Geodata 2018–2021*.

Aporta, Claudio. 2004. "Routes, Trails and Tracks: Trail Breaking among the Inuit of Igloolik." *Études/Inuit/Studies* 28 (2): 9–38. https://doi.org/10.7202/013194ar.

Augé, M. 1995. "Non-Places: Introduction to an Anthropology of Supermodernity." *Journal of the Royal Anthropological Institute* 2 (2). https://doi.org/10.2307/3034109.

Baerenholdt, Jørgen Ole. 2000. "Circumpolar Coping Strategies—Embedding Transnational Cooperation in Local Practices in Greenland?" *Études/Inuit/Studies* 24, (1): 79–96.

Bagrow, L. 1960. *History of Cartography*. Cambridge: Harvard University Press.

Bendixen, Mette, Irina Overeem, Minik T. Rosing, Anders Anker Bjørk, Kurt H. Kjær, Aart Kroon, Gavin Zeitz, and Lars Lønsmann Iversen. 2019. "Promises and Perils of Sand Exploitation in Greenland." *Nature Sustainability* 2; 98–104. https://doi.org/10.1038/s41893-018-0218-6.

Bendsen, Stine, Jesper Nordskilde, and Mads Paabøl Jensen. 2011. "The Transport Commission of Greenland." Association for European Transport and Contributors.

Berry, D. A. 2012. "Cryolite, the Canadian Aluminium Industry and the American Occupation of Greenland during the Second World War." *Polar Journal* 2 (2): 219–235.

Billingsley, James Andrew. 2020. "An Arboretum at the End of an Epoch." *The Avery Review* 46 (April). https://averyreview.com/issues/46/an-arboretum.

Bislev, A., U. Pram Gad, and J.W. Zeuthen. 2018. "China Seeking Arctic Resources—The Arctic Seeking Resources in China." *Arctic Yearbook*.

Bjarløv, S. P., and P. Vladykova. 2011. "The Potential and Need for Energy Saving in Standard Family Detached and Semi-Detached Wooden Houses in Arctic Greenland." *Building and Environment* 46: 1525–1536.

Bjerregaard, Peter, Christina V. L. Larsen, Ivalu K. Sørensen, and Janne S. Tolstrup. 2020. “Alcohol in Greenland 1950–2018: Consumption, Drinking Patterns, and Consequences.” *International Journal of Circumpolar Health* 79, no. 1. https://www.tandfonline.com/doi/full/10.1080/22423982.2020.1814550.

Bosson, J. B., M. Huss, and E. Osipova. 2019. “Disappearing World Heritage Glaciers as a Keystone of Nature Conservation in a Changing Climate.” *Earth's Future* 7, no. 4 (April): 496–479.

Bravo, Michael. 2019. *North Pole—Nature and Culture.* London: Reaktion Books.

Breum, Martin. 2021. “A First-Ever Foreign Policy Opinion Poll in Greenland Shows Support for More Cooperation with US, Denmark.” *Arctic Today* (blog). https://www.arctictoday.com/a-first-ever-foreign-policy-opinion-poll-in-greenland-shows-support-for-more-cooperation-with-us-denmark/.

Brinkley, Bill. 1952. “Birth of a Base.” *LIFE*, September 22.

Bruun, Johanne M. 2018. “Invading the Whiteness: Science, (Sub)Terrain, and US Militarisation of the Greenland Ice Sheet.” *Geopolitics* 25 (1): 167–188. https://doi.org/10.1080/14650045.2018.1543269.

Buijs, Cunera. 2018. “Shared Inuit Culture: European Museums and Arctic Communities.” *Études/Inuit/Studies* 43 (1): 37–59. https://doi.org/10.7202/1064495ar.

Burdett, Ricky, and Adam Kaasa. 2010. “Color and the City.” *New Geographies* 3, special issue, *Urbanisms of Color.*

Bureau of Transportation Statistics. 2020. “Preliminary Estimated Full Year 2019 and December 2019 U.S. Airline Traffic Data.” https://www.bts.gov/newsroom/preliminary-estimated-full-year-2019-and-december-2019-us-airline-traffic-data.

Carruth, Susan Jayne. 2016. “Developing Renewable Energy in Discontiguous Greenland: An Infrastructural Urbanism of Material Practices.” *JoLA—Journal on Landscape Architecture* 11 (1): 66–79. https://doi.org/10.1080/18626033.2016.1144686.

———. 2018. “Place as Progressive Optic: Reflecting on Conceptualisations of Place through a Study of Greenlandic Infrastructures.” In *Future North: The Changing Arctic Landscapes*, 1st ed. London: Routledge.

Charpentier Ljungqvist, Fredrik. 2005. “The Significance of Remote Resource Regions for Norse Greenland.” *Scripta Islandica* 56: 13–54.

Christensen, L., O. A. Nielsen, J. Rich, and M. Knudsen. 2020. “Optimizing Airport Infrastructure for a Country: The Case of Greenland.” *Research in Transportation Economics* 79, no. 4.

Church, M. J., A. J. Dugmore, K. A. Mairs, G. T. Cook, G Sveinbjarnardottir, P. A. Ascough, and K. H. Roucoux. 2007. “Charcoal Production during Norse and Early Medieval Periods in Eyjafjallahreppur, Southern Iceland.” *Radiocarbon* 49 (2): 659–672.

Climate Greenland. n.d. “Agriculture and Forestry.” *Government of Greenland—Ministry of Research and Environment* (blog). http://climategreenland.gl/en/citizen/climate-adaptation/agriculture-and-forestry/.

Cosgrove, D. 2008. *Geography and Vision: Seeing, Imagining and Representing the World.* New York: I. B. Tauris & Co.

Cowen, D., and N. Smith. 2009. “After Geopolitics? From the Geopolitical Social to Geoeconomics.” *Antipode* 41 (1): 22–48.

De Gruyter, Caroline. 2020. "The Lessons of Grøxit." *EUobserver* (blog entry, October 14). https://euobserver.com/opinion/149731.

Denmark, U. E. 2020. "Common Plan for U.S.-Greenland Cooperation in Support of Our Understanding for Pituffik (Thule Air Base)."

Desrochers-Turgeon, Émélie. 2019. "From the Igluvigaq to the Sila: Ceilings in the Inuit Imagination." In *Ceilings and Dreams: The Architecture of Levity*, 1st ed. London: Routledge.

Diamond, Jared. 2003. "Why Do Societies Collapse?" TED Talk. https://www.ted.com/talks/jared_diamond_why_do_societies_collapse?language=en.

Doel, Ronald E. 2016. "Defending the North American Continent: Why the Physical Environmental Sciences Mattered in Cold War Greenland." Pp. 25–46 in *Exploring Greenland: Cold War Science and Technology on Ice*. New York: Palgrave Macmillan.

Doel, Ronald E., Kristine C. Harper, and Matthias Heymann. 2016. *Exploring Greenland—Cold War Science and Technology on Ice*. Palgrave Studies in the History of Science and Technology. New York: Palgrave Macmillan.

Doherty, Gareth. 2010. "Urbanisms of Color." *New Geographies* 3: 2–7.

Dorte Mandrup. 2020. "Ilulissat Icefjord Centre, Greenland." Architecture office website. Accessed May 11. https://www.dortemandrup.dk/work/ilulissat-icefjord-centre-greenland.

Dümpelmann, Sonja, and Charles Waldheim. 2016. *Airport Landscape: Urban Ecologies in the Aerial Age*. Cambridge: Harvard University Graduate School of Design.

Dzik, Anthony J. 2015. "Three Kilometers & Three Centuries: Modernisation and the Cultural Landscape of Kulusuk Island, East Greenland." *Shima: The International Journal of Research into Island Cultures* 9, no. 2.

Edwards, Kevin J., Edward Schofield, and Jette Arneborg. 2010. "Was Erik the Red's 'Brattahli ' Located at Qinngua? A Dissenting View." *Viking and Medieval Scandinavia* 6: 83–99.

Eigen, Edward. 2020. "Histories of Landscape Architecture 1." Syllabus. HIS-4141. Cambridge: Harvard Graduate School of Design.

Elixhauser, Sophie. 2019. "Inuit Responses to Arctic Militarization: Examples from East Greenland." In *Ice and Snow in the Cold War: Histories of Extreme Climatic Environments*. Environment in History: International Perspectives. Berghahn Books.

———. 2018. *Negotiating Personal Autonomy: Communication and Personhood in East Greenland*. Arctic Worlds: Communities, Political Ecology and Ways of Knowing. New York and Oxford: Routledge.

Farish, M., and P.W. Lackenbauer. 2009. "High Modernism in the Arctic: Planning Frobisher Bay and Inuvik." *Journal of Historical Geography* 35 (3): 517–544.

Fleischer, Malu, Michael Nielsen, and Marius Elisasen. 2018. "14.2b.2 Ersersaaneq: Creating Knowledge through Images." *ICASS* IX. https://pur.hypotheses.org/files/2018/06/Book_of_Abstract_ICASS_IX.pdf.

Folger, Tim. 2017. "Why Did Greenland's Vikings Vanish?" *Smithsonian Magazine* (March). https://www.smithsonianmag.com/history/why-greenland-vikings-vanished-180962119/.

Foster, Sheila R., and Christian Iaione. 2016. "The City as a Commons." *Yale Law & Policy Review*, 282–349.

GEUS. 2021. "The Land of the 'Icefjord People.'" *GEUS—Geological Survey of Denmark and Greenland* (blog). https://eng.geus.dk/explore-geology/learning-about-geology/explore-ilulissat-icefjord/the-land-of-the-'icefjord-people'.

Government of Greenland. 2020. "Politics in Greenland." https://naalakkersuisut.gl/en/About-government-of-greenland/About-Greenland/Politics-in-Greenland.

Grønlands Nationalmuseum & Arkiv. 2021. Museum exhibition, Nuuk.

Grønnow, B. 1986. "Recent Archaeological Investigations of West Greenland Caribou Hunting." *Arctic Anthropology* 23 (1/2): 57–80.

Grydehøj, Adam. 2014. "Constructing a Centre on the Periphery: Urbanization and Urban Design in the Island City of Nuuk, Greenland." *Island Studies Journal* 9, no. 2 (November): 205–222.

———. 2020. "Unravelling Economic Dependence and Independence in Relation to Island Sovereignty: The Case of Kalaallit Nunaat (Greenland)." *Island Studies Journal* 15 (1): 89–112. https://doi.org/10.24043/isj.101.

Gulløv, Hans Christian. 2004. *Nunarput, Vort Land—Thulekulturen.* Grønlands Forhistorie. Copenhagen, Denmark: Gyldendal A/S.

Hall, R. 2015. *The Transparent Traveler: The Performance and Culture of Airport Security.* Durham, NC: Duke University Press.

Hansen, Klaus Georg. 2021. "Greenlandic Visions for a Freer Greenland." Paper presented at the conference "Imagining Independence in the Arctic," *ICASS* X (June 18).

———. 2021. Greenland as a complex cultural, interconnected, and geographical space. Zoom meeting (April 26).

Hemmersam, Peter. 2016. "Arctic Architectures." *Polar Record* 52 (265): 412–422.

———. 2021. *Making the Arctic City.* London: Bloomsbury.

Herrero, Nieves, and Sharon R. Roseman. 2015. *The Tourism Imaginary and Pilgrimages to the Edges of the World.* Bristol: Channel View Publications.

Hersher, Rebecca. 2016. "Numbers Lie Even More Than Usual in Greenland." *NPR* (blog). https://www.npr.org/sections/goatsandsoda/2016/04/21/475003055/numbers-lie-even-more-than-usual-in-greenland.

Heymann, M., H. Knudsen, M. L. Lolck, H. Nielsen, and C. J. Ries. 2010. "Exploring Greenland: Science and Technology in Cold War Settings." *Canadian Journal of the History of Science, Technology and Medicine* 33 (2): 11–42.

Høegh, Kenneth, and Birgitte Jacobson. 2021. "The Forest Plantations in the Greenlandic Arboretum." *Department of Geosciences and Natural Resource Management* (blog). https://ign.ku.dk/english/about/arboreta/arboretum-greenland/forest-plantations.

Hook, Leslie. 2019. "Boom Town: Greenland's Climate Change Gold Rush." *Financial Times*, sec. FT Magazine: Life and Arts.

Hunt, Andrew. "Ilulissat Icefjord." 2014. Pp. 377–78 in *Antarctica and the Arctic Circle: A Geographic Encyclopedia of the Earth's Polar Regions.*

Ilulissat Icefjord Centre. 2021. Museum exhibition, Ilulissat.

Ingels, Bjarke. 2011. "National Gallery of Greenland by BIG." *Dezeen* (blog). https://www.dezeen.com/2011/02/11/national-gallery-of-greenland-by-big/.

Ingold, Tim. 1993. "The Temporality of the Landscape." *World Archaeology—Conceptions of Time and Ancient Society* 25 (2): 152–174.

Ioannides, D. 2019. "Greenland's Tourism

Policy Making and the Risk of Overtourism." In *Overtourism: Excesses, Discontents and Measures in Travel and Tourism*. Wallingford, Oxfordshire, and Boston: CABI.

Jessen, Søren, Hanne D. Holmslykke, Kristine Rasmussen, Niels Richard, and Peter E. Holm. n.d. "Hydrology and Pore Water Chemistry in a Permafrost Wetland, Ilulissat, Greenland." *Water Resource Research* 50. https://doi.org/10.1002/2013WR014376.

Kaae, B.C. 2006. "Greenland/Kalaallit Nunaat." Pp. 101–112 in *Extreme Tourism: Lessons from the World's Cold Water Islands*. Oxford: Elsevier.

———. 2002. "Nature and Tourism in Greenland." Pp. 43–53 in *Wilderness in the Circumpolar North: Searching for Compatibility in Ecological, Traditional, and Ecotourism Values*.

Kaján, Eva. n.d. "Arctic Tourism and Sustainable Adaptation: Community Perspectives to Vulnerability and Climate Change." *Scandinavian Journal of Hospitality and Tourism* 14, no. (1): 60–79.

Kalaallit Airports. "The New Airport at Ilulissat," 2020. https://kair.gl/en/Ilulissat.

KHR. 2020. "KHR Vinder Konkurrence Om Ny Skole i Centrum Af Nuuk / KHR Wins the Competition for a New School in the Centre of Nuuk." *KHR Architecture* (blog). https://khr.dk/news/khr-vinder-konkurrence-om-ny-skole-i-centrum-af-nuuk-khr-wins-competition-new-school-centre.

KNR Greenlandic Broadcasting Corporation. 2010. "Blok P-Beboere Vil Ikke Til Qinngorput," November 16, 2010.

Kommuneqarfik Sermersooq. 2019. "Planstrategie P18." Nuuk: Afdeling for By- og Boligudvikling.

Kristjánsson, Jónas. 2005. *The First Settler of the New World: The Vinland Expedition of Thorfinn Karlsefni*. Reykjavik: University of Iceland Press.

Kromann, Virna. 2019. "Oprydning Efter Amerikanerne: 10.000 Rustne Olietønder Er Samlet Sammen." September 4, 2019. https://knr.gl/da/nyheder/oprydning-efter-amerikanerne-10000-rustne-olietønder-er-samlet-sammen.

Lam, Anita, and Matthew Tegelberg. 2020. "Dark Tourism in Iceberg Alley: The Hidden Ecological Costs of Consuming Iceberg Deaths." In *Criminal Anthroposcenes*. Palgrave Studies in Crime.

Landslægeembedet. 2021. "Følg smittespredningen af ny coronavirus, COVID-19." COVID-19 Statistik. Landslægeembedet, January 2021. https://nun.gl/Emner/Borgere/Coronavirus_emne/Foelg_smittespredningen.

Larsen, F. B. 1992. "The Quiet Life of a Revolution: Greenlandic Home Rule 1979–1992." *Études/Inuit/Studies* 16 (1/2): 199–226.

Larsen, H. E., and J. Meldgaard. 1958. "Paleo-Eskimo Cultures in Disko Bugt, West Greenland." *Meddelelser Om Grønland* 161 (2).

Laruelle, Marlene. n.d. "The Three Waves of Arctic Urbanisation. Drivers, Evolutions, Prospects." *Polar Record* 55: 1–12.

Lemelin, H., J. Dawson, E. J. Stewart, P. Maher, and M. Lück. 2010. "Last-Chance Tourism: The Boom, Doom, and Gloom of Visiting Vanishing Destinations." *Current Issues in Tourism* 13: 477–493.

Lindsey, Gillian. 2005. "Ilulissat." In *Encyclopedia of the Arctic*. New York and London: Routledge.

Loovers, Jan Peter Laurens. 2020. "Southern Ambitions." In *Arctic Culture and Climate*. London: Thames & Hudson.

Løvstrøm, Qivioq Nivi. 2021. "Greenland as a Complex Cultural,

Interconnected, and Geographical Space. Zoom meeting, April 26.

Lynnerup, Niels. 2015. "The Thule Inuit Mummies from Greenland." *he Anatomical Record* 298: 1001–1006. https://doi.org/10.1002/ar.23131.

Martin-Nielsen, J. 2012. "The Other Cold War: The United States and Greenland's Ice Sheet Environment, 1948–1966." *Journal of Historical Geography* 38 (1): 69–80.

Mellor, Malcolm. 1968. "Methods of Building on Permanent Snowfields." Cold Regions Science and Engineering Laboratory (CRREL).

Milius, Susan. 2000. "Red Snow, Green Snow." *Science News* 157 (21): 328–330.

Ministry of Finance. 2020. "Political and Economic Report." Nuuk.

Møller, Eva B., and Tove Lading. 2020. "Current Building Strategies in Greenland." *E3S Web of Conferences* 172. https://doi.org/10.1051/e3sconf/202017219004.

Nielsen, Kristian H. 2016. "Small State Preoccupations: Science and Technology in the Pursuit of Modernization, Security, and Sovereignty in Greenland." In *Exploring Greenland—Cold War Science and Technology on Ice*. Palgrave Studies in the History of Science and Technology. New York: Palgrave Macmillan.

Nordatlantens Brygge. 2013. "Block P—The Final Tribute." https://www.nordatlantens.dk/en/exhibitions/blok-p-in-nuuk/.

Nordatlantisk Byggeri. 2018. "KHR Architecture:Vi Er Blevet Bidt Af Grønland." *Bygge- & Anlægsavisen* (blog). https://bygge-anlaegsavisen.dk/khr-architecture-vi-er-blevet-bidt-af-groenland.

Nuttall, Mark. 1992. *Arctic Homeland: Kinship, Community and Development in Northwest Greenland*. Toronto: University of Toronto Press.

———. 2017. *Climate, Society, and Subsurface Politics in Greenland: Under the Great Ice*. London: Routledge.

———. 2009. "Living in a World of Movement: Human Resilience to Human Instability in Greenland." Pp. 292–310 in *Anthropology and Climate Change*.

Nuuk City Development A/S. 2018. "Siorarsiorfik." https://ncd.gl/en/The-Project/Homes.

Olesen, Simon Mølhom. 2019. "The Danish Decolonisation of Greenland, 1945–54." *Aarhus University* (blog entry, August 19). https://nordics.info/en/show/artikel/the-danish-decolonisation-of-greenland-1945-54-1/.

Palma, David, et al. 2019. "Cruising the Marginal Ice Zone: Climate Change and Arctic Tourism." *Polar Geography* 42 (4): 215–235.

Pendlebury, J., M. Short, and A. While. 2009. "Urban World Heritage Sites and the Problem of Authenticity." *Cities* 26 (6): 349–358.

Peschardt, Sofie. n.d. "Nuuk City Development." Official website Nordic Office of Architecture. https://nordicarch.com/project/nuuk-city-development.

Petersen, N. 2011. "SAC at Thule: Greenland in the U.S. Polar Strategy." *Journal of Cold War Studie* 13 (2): 90–115. https://doi.org/10.1162/JCWS_a_00138.

Peterson, Ivars. 1983. "Blue Snow and Green Ice." *Science News* 123 (23): 364–365.

Qujaukitsoq, Vittus. 2018. Foreword to *National Strategy of Geodata 2018–2021*.

Rahbek-Clemmensen, J., and L. J. Nielsen. 2020. "The Middleman—The Driving Forces behind Denmark's Arctic Policy." Pp. 77–96 in *Handbook on Geopolitics and Security in the Arctic*. Switzerland: Springer Nature.

Rasmussen, Knud. 1927. *Across Arctic America: Narrative of the Fifth Thule Expedition*. New York: G. P. Putnam's Sons.

Rasmussen, Lars Løkke. 2018. "Løkke: Selvstændigt Grønland Skal Klare Sig Selv Økonomisk." *Sermitsiaq AG*. https://sermitsiaq.ag/loekke-selvstaendigt-groenland-klare-oekonomisk.

Rundstrom, Robert A. 1990. "A Cultural Interpretation of Inuit Map Accuracy." *Geographical Review* 80, no. 2 (April): 155–168.

Schaberg, C. 2011. *The Textual Life of Airports*. London: Bloomsbury.

Schrot, O. G., J. H. Christensen, and H. Formayer. 2019. "Greenland Winter Tourism in a Changing Climate." *Journal of Outdoor Recreation and Tourism* 27. https://doi.org/10.1016/j.jort.2019.100224.

Sejersen, Frank. 2007. "Indigenous Urbanism Revisited—The Case of Greenland." *Indigenous Affairs* 3: 26–31.

Sermitsiaq. 2010. "Blok P-beboere genhuses i Qinngorput." *Sermitsiaq AG* (February). https://archive.is/20120718061631/http://sermitsiaq.ag/indland/article110015.ece#selection-655.0-655.36.

Sheppard, Lola, and Mason White. 2017. *Many Norths: Spatial Practice in a Polar Territory*. New York: Actar Publishers.

Sigurdsson, Haraldur. 1984. "Some Landmarks in Icelandic Cartography down to the End of the Sixteenth Century." *Arctic* 37 (4): 389–401.

Simonetti, Christán, and Tim Ingold. 2018. "Ice and Concrete: Solid Fluids of Environmental Change." *Journal of Contemporary Archaeology* 5 (1): 19–31.

Smárason, Hjörtur. 2021. Ilulissat Icefjord Centre." Booklet Kangiata Illorsua—Ilulissat Icefjord Centre.

Smed, Karina M. 2017. "Role of 'Culture' in the Destination of Ilulissat, Greenland." In *Tourism and Indigeneity in the Arctic*. Blue Ridge Summit, PA: Channel View Publications.

———. 2014. "The Culture of Nature: Destination Visitability in Ilulissat, Greenland." *Northern Review* 38: 269–293.

Sørensen, Jane Buus, and Ulla Willumsen. 2013. "Housing Issues in Nuuk (Greenland) and How to Get Students Involved." *Études/Inuit/Studies* 37 (1): 175. https://doi.org/10.7202/1025260ar.

Sørensen, M. 2010. "The Archaeology of Old Nuulliit: Eigil Knuth's Investigations in the Thule Region, North Greenland, 1952–1990." Copenhagen: Museum Tusculanum Press, University of Copenhagen.

Statistics Greenland. 2020. "Population 2020." Grønlands Statistik—Statistics Greenland, December 2, 2020. http://www.stat.gl/publ/en/BE/202001/pdf/Population%202020.pdf.

Steering group for Ilulissat Icefjord. n.d. "Management Plan for Ilulissat Icefjord 2018–2020." UNESCO. https://www.google.com/url?sa=t&rct=j&q=&esrc=s&source=web&cd=&ved=2ahUKEwjHwPuDjuzvAhU3hP0HHW5FDIwQFjAAegQIAxAD&url=https%3A%2F%2Fwhc.unesco.org%2Fdocument%2F171549&usg=AOvVaw0fzbAOufhx_8DcKj9KVKCq.

Stoler, A. L. 2008. "Imperial Debris: Reflections on Ruins and Ruination." *Cultural Anthropology* 23 (2): 191–219.

Stone, P. R., and R. Sharpley. 2008. "Consuming Dark Tourism: A Thanatological Perspective." *Annals of Tourism Research* 35 (2): 574–595.

Sutherland, Patricia D. 2000. "The Norse and Native North Americans." Pp. 238–247 *Vikings: The North Atlantic Saga*, edited by William W. Fitzhugh and Elisabeth I. Ward. Washington,

DC: Smithsonian Institution Press.

Sværd, Runa, Nuuk's head of planning. 2021. Interview by the author.

Sveinbjörnsdóttir, J. B. 2015. "Underneath the Shieldshaped Mountain, the Helicopter, and the Sun: A Visual Ethnography with the Children in Kulusuk, East Greenland." *Journal of Visual and Media Anthropology* 1 (1): 32–64.

Swirnoff, Lois. 2000. *The Color of Cities: An International Perspective.* New York: McGraw-Hill.

Taagholt, Jørgen. 1991. "The Early History of Greenland." *History of Earth Sciences Society,* special Arctic issue 10 (2): 247–258.

Takahashi, M., ed. 2019. "Greenland's Quest for Autonomy and the Political Dynamics Surrounding the Thule Air Base." Pp. 25–50 in *The Influence of Security on National Sub-State Actors: Using Military Bases to Forge Autonomy.* Springer Polar Sciences.

Tejsner, Pelle. 2017. "Indigenous Modes of Ownership: Reopening the Case for Communal Rights in Greenland." In *Governance of Arctic Offshore Oil and Gas,* 1st ed. Routledge.

Thisted, Kirsten. 2015. "Pioneering Nation: New Narratives about Greenland and Greenlanders Launched through Arts and Branding." Pp. 22–38 in *The New Arctic.* Switzerland: Springer International Publishing.

Tommasini, D. 2014. "Tourism, Human Capital & Regional Development in Three Communities in Greenland: Tourism in Greenland: Ukkusissat, Narsaq and Qaanaaq." *Arctic Yearbook.*

Uhre, Kjerstin, and Knut Eirik Dahl. 2017. "Envisioning Dialogues of New Urban Landscapes in Nuuk." *Creative Approaches to Planning and Local Development—Insights from Small and Medium-Sized Towns in Europe,* 1st ed. London: Routledge.

Urry, John. 1992. "The Tourist Gaze and the 'Environment.'" *Theory, Culture & Society* 9, no. 3 (August): 1–26. https://doi.org/10.1177/026327692009003001.

Vindum, Kjeld, and Adrian Täckman. 2012. "Grønland Revisited / Greenland Revisited." *Arkitektens Forlag.*

Visit Greenland. 2017. "Tourism Statistics Report 2016." Nuuk.

———. 2019. "Tourism Statistics Report 2019."

———. 2020. "Towards More Tourism: A Joint Effort for Growth, Innovation and Responsible Tourism." https://traveltrade.visitgreenland.com/wp-content/uploads/2020/02/Strategi-EN-060220-booklet.pdf.

Warmann, Catherine. 2010. "House of Families by Fantastic Norway." *Dezeen* (blog entry, December 2). https://www.dezeen.com/2010/12/02/house-of-families-by-fantastic-norway/.

Whitridge, Peter. 2002. "Landscapes, Houses, Bodies, Things: A Place and the Archaeology of the Inuit Imaginary." Society for American Archaeology, 67th annual meeting, Denver, CO.

Williams, R. 1993. "Cultural Origins and Environmental Implications of Large Technological Systems." *Science in Context* 6 (2): 377–403.

Wills, Matthew. 2015. "The Surprising Colors of Snow." *JSTOR Daily* (blog).

World Heritage Committee. 2004. "Decisions Adopted at the 28th Session of the World Heritage Commitee in Suzhou, China." Suzhou, China: UNESCO.

Biographies

Bert De Jonghe is a Belgian landscape architect, the founder of Transpolar Studio, and a Doctor of Design student at Harvard University. He earned his Master in Design Studies degree (with a concentration in Urbanism, Landscape, and Ecology) at the Harvard University Graduate School of Design after completing a Master of Landscape Architecture at the Oslo School of Architecture and Design. Previously, he worked together with Harvard GSD's Office for Urbanization and with landscape architecture offices in Belgium, South Africa, and Norway. De Jonghe's recent publications include a co-authored article, "The opening of the Transpolar Sea Route: Logistical, geopolitical, environmental, and socioeconomic impacts," published in the peer-reviewed Marine Policy journal.

Charles Waldheim is a North American architect and urbanist. Waldheim's research examines the relations between landscape, ecology, and contemporary urbanism. He is author, editor, or co-editor of numerous books on these subjects, and his writing has been published and translated internationally. Waldheim is John E. Irving Professor at Harvard University's Graduate School of Design where he directs the School's Office for Urbanization. Waldheim is recipient of the Rome Prize Fellowship from the American Academy in Rome; the Visiting Scholar Research Fellowship at the Study Centre of the Canadian Centre for Architecture; the Cullinan Chair at Rice University; and the Sanders Fellowship at the University of Michigan.

Mia M. Bennett is an assistant professor in the Department of Geography at the University of Hong Kong. Through fieldwork and remote sensing, she researches the geopolitics of development in northern frontiers, namely the Arctic, Russian Far East, and along the more remote corridors of China's Belt and Road Initiative. Mia received a PhD in Geography from the University of California, Los Angeles, where she was a National Science Foundation Graduate Research Fellow, and an MPhil in Polar Studies from the University of Cambridge, where she was a Gates Scholar. She has published extensively in academic and public outlets and edits a long-running blog on the Arctic at cryopolitics.com.

Image Credits

	Pages
Ammassalik map by David Trood. Satellite image from Google Earth. Collage by Bert De Jonghe, 2021.	65
Aningaaq Rosing Carlsen (Visit Greenland), Unsplash, 2019.	70
Aningaaq Rosing Carlsen (Visit Greenland), Unsplash, 2021.	68-69, 72, 74-75, 76-77, & 102
Annie Spratt, Unsplash, 2018.	110-111
Jon Arnold, Alamy license, 2015.	94
Bent Helmudt, 1951. Courtesy of the Danish Arctic Institute.	26
Bert De Jonghe, 2017.	42, 61, 98 & 105
Bert De Jonghe & Dirk De Jonghe, 2021.	30, 32, 36-37, 38, 73, 83, 85, 86, 91, 114-115, 118, 119, 120, 122-123, 124, 126, 128-129, 130-131 & 132-133
Bert De Jonghe, 2022	45, 58-59 & 107
Dahl & Uhre Arkitekter (Tromsø), TNT Nuuk (Nuuk), Asplan Viak landscape (Oslo), MDH Arkitekter (Oslo), Fantastic Norway (Oslo), 42 Architects + Regional Associates (London), and M:ARC and Arkitekti (Nuuk).	82
Filip Gielda, (Visit Greenland), Unsplash, 2016.	112-113
Filip Gielda, (Visit Greenland), Unsplash, 2019.	103, 104 & 108-109
Finn Samson, 1965. Courtesy of the Danish Arctic Institute.	29
Inger Oxholm Campsie, 1967. Courtesy of the Danish Arctic Institute.	80

Jette Bang, 1961. Courtesy of the Danish Arctic Institute. © SABAM Belgium 2021.	50, 52, 53, 56 & 66
Adam Mork, Alamy license, 2007.	92
NASA/Goddard Space Flight Center Scientific Visualization Studio (Led by Cindy Starr, 2012). Topographic data is the courtesy of Ian Howat, The Ohio State University, Columbus, OH. The MOG mosaic (MODIS) is courtesy of T. Scambos, NSDIC, Boulder, CO.	23
NASA's Earth Observing-1 satellite, 2006.	46-47
Svend Lauge Koch, 1916. Courtesy of the Danish Arctic Institute.	62, Left
Therkel Mathiassen, 1921. Courtesy of the Danish Arctic Institute.	62, Right

Inventing Greenland
Designing an Arctic Nation

Published by
Actar Publishers,
New York, Barcelona
www.actar.com

Author
Bert De Jonghe

Edited by
Bert De Jonghe

Graphic Design
Actar Publishers

Copy editing and proofreading
Mia Bennett and Elizabeth Kugler

Printing and binding
Arlequin

Distribution
Actar D, Inc. New York, Barcelona.

New York
440 Park Avenue South,
17th Floor
New York, NY 10016, USA
T +1 212 966 2207
salesnewyork@actar-d.com

Barcelona
Roca i Batlle 2-4
08023 Barcelona, SP
T +34 933 282 183
eurosales@actar-d.com

Indexing
ISBN: 978-1-638409-89-2
PCN: Library of Congress Control Number: 2021947734

Printed in Europe.

Publication date: March 2022.

This book has been produced sustainably, using PEFC - Certified wood-free paper and soy-based ink and recycled carboard for the cover.